Account For Your Own Success

Everything You Need to Manage Your Own Business and Personal Finances

By Dan Meyer

Account For Your Own Success discusses common laws and regulations that affect individuals and small businesses. Naturally, this information is subject to change and must be used keeping this fact in mind. An attempt has been made to provide a digest of conventional wisdom regarding management of personal finances. These suggestions are likewise subject to change and offered only as a general guide, and not as a substitute for obtaining complete and timely information prior to making financial decisions.

Cover and Chapter Page Illustrations
by Dixon Brady

Published by
Management Communications Systems, Inc.
Charlotte, North Carolina

Ordering Information:

MCS, Inc.
PO Box 4884
Alexandria, Virginia 22303

ISBN: 0-932150-04-7

Library of Congress Catalog Card Number:
92-61246

Printed on Recycled Paper in
The United States of America

For Walter T. Meyer

An intelligent, self-educated and gentle man who taught me by example the value of hard work, organization and thrift. This book is dedicated with love and admiration to my father.

Preface

There are plenty of books that promise to make accounting simple, but I found the double-entry system they describe was more complicated than I needed for my small, start-up business. The few books featuring a single-entry system were long on forms and short on instructions. *And that's why this book fully explains the use of one, simple, multipurpose form.*

I'll admit that when it comes to recordkeeping, I'm lazy. So I was searching for something that was as efficient as it was easy; *And that's why this book shows you how to minimize the time spent keeping the books.*

As a small business owner I needed to know how to manage money as well as how to keep track of it. But accounting books don't often address important financial management questions. *And that's why this book shows you how to prepare budgets, cash flows, inventories, and tax returns.*

Financial management books tend to focus either on business or personal finances. For sole-proprietors the two are usually inseparable. *And that's why this book discusses both business and personal finances, and shows you how to apply business techniques to improve your personal finances.*

In sum, I couldn't find a book that concisely answered all the financial questions I had when I started my business. I reasoned that others who are starting, or even just considering, their own business had the same need. *And that's why this book...*

Contents

Contents

Businesses seldom fail from sudden events, but rather from a gradual squeeze on profits. This chapter shows how you can monitor and maintain your profit margin.

The P&L Statement... The Balance Sheet... The Budget... Cash Flow Projection... Just-In-Time Inventory Management... Valuation Of The Business...

This chapter explains how the tools and techniques used to manage your business finances can be used to successfully manage your personal finances.

Personal Financial Summary... Increasing Your Savings Rate... Budgeting... Finding Your Net Worth... Meeting Short Term and Retirement Goals... Investment Options... Financial Planning...

Appendix

chapter 1

gearing up

What Will I Learn From This Book?

The purpose of this book is to encourage you to be your own financial expert. It explains how you can profit from:

- keeping and using financial records

- having a sideline business

- applying business methods to personal finances.

The book assumes you know nothing about financial management and will teach you a simple, yet powerful recordkeeping system that is ideally suited to managing your small business and personal finances. A realistic example is incorporated to show exactly how each transaction is recorded, and how to use your records to maximize earnings and file worry free tax returns.

What's So Important About Records?

Records are the life-blood of your financial health. Good records will:

- establish your legitimacy

- help you make sound financial decisions

- support your requests for credit and financing

- establish the value of the business.

Why Do I Need To Learn How to Keep the Records?

Recordkeeping is a chore and it's tempting to let someone else worry about it. But this could be a very costly mistake. The best reason for keeping your own records is that *no one knows more or cares more about your business and personal finances than you do.* Secondly, inadequate financial records are a major cause of business failures, so this is a task worth mastering. Lastly, professional help is costly and unfortunately not always provided with *only your* best interests in mind.

In time, you can confidently assign recordkeeping chores to someone else because you'll have the knowledge that comes from having done the job yourself; you'll know what the figures mean and how to use the information to maximize your income.

If you decide to use tax preparers, you'll know what they should be doing and will minimize the cost because you'll supply all the necessary figures.

Why Should I Consider A Sideline Business?

Current studies by the Tax Foundation show that 30% of the income earned by the typical American family goes to pay income-related taxes; 20% federal and 10% state. It is by far the single biggest expense in the family budget. The studies show that the *necessities of life* comprise only 33%; food 11%, shelter 17% and clothing 5%. It's easy to see why it's so important to learn about and use whatever tax breaks are available.

There are fewer tax breaks than there used to be, but the biggest - operating your own business - is still intact. What's more, since small business is central to our free enterprise system and accounts for 7 out of 10 new jobs, it's likely that tax law will continue to favor the creation, operation and expansion of small businesses.

What Tax Breaks Does A Small Business Offer?

Operating a small business offers the following tax benefits:

- retirement contributions above your IRA and employer plan limits;

- deduction of interest, depreciation, taxes and operating costs of business property including business use of personal residence and auto;

- deduction of meals, travel and educational expenses needed to maintain and grow the business;

- deduction of personal and professional services including salaries of family members working in the business.

How Do I Legally Establish A Business?

There are surprisingly few legal requirements needed to start a business, and all can be met without the assistance of an attorney.

■ Form of Business - You have to decide what the legal form of your business will be. The choices are:

Partnership
S-Corporation
C-Corporation
Sole Proprietorship

The sole proprietorship is the simplest form of business, requiring the least paperwork and expense. A sole proprietorship is usually the best choice for starting a sideline business and is used in our example. Incidently, businesses owned and operated by a husband and wife qualify as a sole proprietorship. Detailed descriptions of the forms of business with their advantages and disadvantages are found in Appendix a.

■ Business Name, Licenses, Zoning - If you are going to operate the business in a name other than your own, you'll need to file a fictitious name statement. Contact your county clerk's office for specifics. While there, ask about and apply for any licenses that may be required for your business. Usually the costs for filing a name and business license are small. If you plan to operate out of your home, make sure the business complies with zoning laws.

■ Financial Records Required - The legal requirements concerning financial records specify only that they be permanent, accurate, and complete. Depending on your form of business, you may also have a choice as to the following options:

■ Calendar or Fiscal Year? - Financial records must be kept on a twelve month basis. At one time small businesses could choose when their business year would begin and end. However, sole proprietors and most small businesses are required to use the calendar year (January 1-December 31). This actually simplifies bookkeeping since all federal, state, and local tax reporting is based on the calendar year.

Timing the start of a small business can be a helpful tax-planning tool. For example, normal start up business losses can often be used to offset salaries and other earnings for that year and reduce the total amount of tax due. Owners can control future business earnings by timing their billings and their spending.

■ Cash or Accrual Method? - The cash method means that income is recorded *when*

you receive payment, and expenses are recorded *when you pay them*. In the accrual method, income is recorded *when the income is earned (when you bill someone)* and expenses are recorded when *you receive the goods or service (when you get a bill from someone)*. The cash method is much simpler and is permitted for businesses earning less than $5 million per year. However, if the business involves selling from an inventory of goods, the IRS insists that the accrual method be used. Even then, you are allowed to use the cash method throughout the year and "bring records to accrual" by simply adding any uncollected and unpaid bills as of December 31; this method is called modified accrual.

■ Single Entry or Double Entry? - A single entry system means every dollar transaction is recorded only once—either as income, an expense, an asset (something you own) or a liability (something you owe). It is a simple system ideally suited to small business and even recommended by the IRS. It's important to understand that the single entry system is every bit as accurate as the more complicated "double entry" system. The double entry system gets its name from the fact that *two entries* are made for every transaction; that is, one account is *credited* with the given dollar amount and a second account is *debited* an equal dollar amount. While this system offers certain advantages, it generally requires a semester of course work and considerable practice to master. For most small businesses, the benefits simply don't offset the additional time and expense double entry systems require.

Why Do I Need A Business Bank Account?

Financial recordkeeping boils down to keeping track of dollars that come in, dollars that go out, and dollars that are left. That's exactly what a bank account does for you—accurately and at reasonable cost. The recordkeeping materials and services a bank provides include:

- income record (deposit slips)
- expense record (checks)
- monthly summary (bank statement)
- record storage and retrieval (microfilm)
- credit reference (for you and your business).

How Can I Keep Business Records Trouble-Free?

- Open and use only *one* business bank account.
- Deposit *all* business income in this account.
- Pay *all* business bills by check from this account.
- *Never* withhold cash from deposits.
- *Never* use this account for personal expenses.
- Check the bank statement soon after it arrives.

What Should I Look For In A Business Bank Account?

Ideally, your checking account should have the following features:

- Pays interest (permitted for sole -proprietorships)
- Free checking (if minimum balance is maintained)
- Overdraft privilege (bank covers your overdrafts)
- Statement dates near the beginning and end of month
- Canceled checks listed in numerical order.

If you expect to write less than 30 checks per month, consider the "3-Up" business checks *with duplicates* (3 checks per page). If you'll be writing more than 30 checks a month, consider getting a "One-Write" system (see Appendix 1).

What Other Services Provide Useful, Low-Cost Records?

- Credit Cards — If you expect to be doing any travel or entertaining in connection with furthering your business (and it's hard to imagine that you wouldn't), you'll want a credit card such as VISA or Master Card. Credit cards are a virtual necessity when traveling. You can hardly rent a car or confirm a hotel reservation without one. Besides, it's not smart to carry the amount of cash needed for the average business trip. A credit card allows you to get a cash advance from any bank, eliminating the hassle of cashing an out-of-state check. And, as if these conveniences weren't enough, you get a dated, itemized receipt for each purchase, a detailed summary each month, and an annual summary by major expense category. If you plan to do a lot of traveling and entertaining, you may want the card in the business name and restrict its use to business expenses only. Otherwise, you can use your personal credit card and simply note the business purpose on the credit card slip when you sign it.

You pay little or nothing for these services provided you pay the entire balance due each month. Otherwise, such conveniences will cost you dearly because of the high interest rates on credit card balances. If you can't pay the balance off each month, or if this is the only credit you can get, take it as a sign that something's wrong and get help. The National Foundation of Consumer Credit in Silver Spring, Maryland [(301) 589-5600] coordinates work of hundreds of non-profit counselling centers and can usually arrange for no-cost assistance.

▪ Telephone Companies supply itemized monthly listings of calls and costs. These detailed records not only document your expenses they are also helpful in analyzing phone usage and controlling costs. Some companies will provide detailed analyses of usage and suggest ways to lower costs. If your business involves a lot of telephoning, you'll want a separate line and discount long distance services.

▪ Suppliers can reduce your bookkeeping by providing you with summaries showing quantities, prices and dates of your orders. Such records help you control inventories, prepare budgets and compare costs.

▪ Loan Makers provide annual statements showing interest payments and loan balances which are very helpful in preparing tax returns and balance sheets.

What Bookkeeping Equipment Will I Need?

To assure speed and accuracy, you'll want a simple ten-key adding machine.

FIGURE 1 Ten Key Adding Machine

You're often better off with a used, good quality machine rather than a cheap new one. Make sure it uses standard 2 1/4" tape. Larger stationery stores often have used machines and will usually also service them.

You'll also need a four drawer (or 2 two-drawer) file cabinet(s). Full suspension cabinets provides more room and easier access than inexpensive cabinets; and suspension file folders are well worth their small additional cost. Keep your space limitations in mind: bigger cabinets are not necessarily better. If you don't already have a desk, an efficient work space can be made by putting a laminated desk top (24"x54") over 2 two-drawer cabinets. Look in stationery stores and local classified ads under "office equipment" for used file cabinets. A fire-proof box for safekeeping negotiable checks and other important papers is inexpensive and also recommended.

All the recordkeeping forms you need are included in this book and may be photocopied for your personal use as needed. The beauty and simplicity of this system is that the entire year's financial records are on 5 letter-size sheets of paper (an annual and four quarterly summaries).

If your business is primarily retail sales involving mostly cash transactions, you'll want to invest in a cash register that produces a *two-part tape* and *subtotals sales tax and sales by major product*. Such machines are much less expensive than they use to be, and you can often find good used or reconditioned machines. If you have a moderate amount of cash transactions you can get by with the familiar *2-part cash receipt forms*, which come in bound books or folded for loading into mechanical dispensers.

On the other hand, if your business is based on billing clients or customers after your product or service is delivered, you'll want to purchase *pre-printed, numbered, two-part invoice forms and matching double window envelopes*, which will more than pay for themselves in time saved.

You'll minimize the time spent on recordkeeping if you have a pleasant, quiet area with everything you need within easy reach. The space should be large enough to keep all your financial records and have a well lighted work surface with enough room for your papers and desk accessories.

e𝓰 *Impressed with the advantages offered by a sideline business, we decide to start one. We plan to sell instructional books and consulting services on ways to save money. Our business name will be EconoGuides which we file with the county after determining there is no other business operating under that name.*

We select sole proprietorship as our legal form because of the simplicity and the control it offers, and because the business will not involve high risk of injury —where the protection offered by the corporate form would be more advisable. Selection of the sole proprietorship form makes our business year the same as the calendar year.

The decision to sell a product (books) means that we have to use the accrual method of recordkeeping. We select the modified method which will allow us to operate on the easier cash method throughout the year, and bring the records to accrual by a one time entry of any outstanding income or unpaid bills as of December 31. In our state, the decision to sell a product also means we need a business license and that we will have to collect the state sales tax on our product sales.

After some comparison shopping, we open a business checking account in the name of EconoGuides. The account is interest bearing, offers free checking with a minimum balance and has overdraft privileges. Having taken care of the necessary preliminaries, we are ready to transact business. We will describe how each transaction is recorded and used in italicized passages headed by the company logo: e𝓰

money coming in

What Are The Major Ways Money Enters A Business?

Money enters a business in one of four ways:

- sale of products and services
- interest and rents
- loans
- contributions by owner

Your records must show the amount of income from each of these sources. It's usually a good idea to separate "product" and "service" income because they are often taxed differently. It's important to note that loans and owner contributions to the business are not taxable income.

How Many Income Categories Should I Have?

In general, you want the fewest number of income categories that will allow you to track the major sources of income. The following income categories will work for most businesses:

Products: Income from sale of products.

Services: Fees earned from labor.

Interest: Interest earned on funds in the business bank account and other investments.

Sales Tax: Tax collected on sales as required by state law (check applicability).

Misc: Miscellaneous income such as refunds or rebates from suppliers or refunds of previous bank charges.

Non-taxable: Owner contributions, loans or cash advances from bank or other sources.

Naturally, you can modify any of the above categories as needed to reflect your business operations.

How Do Bank Deposit Slips Serve As Income Records?

Since all income must be deposited, the bank deposit slips also serve as the income record making a separate listing unnecessary. All that's needed is to note the income category on the top of each slip (see Figures 2 and 3). Using the larger type slips and a carbon provides ample room and a duplicate copy of each deposit.

At the end of the month, the duplicate slips are stapled together by category and totaled (Figure 4). The category totals are entered on a Financial Summary (Figure 5), and the deposit slips are filed in 9" X 12" envelope labeled with the month and year.

An advantage of using the deposit slips as the income record is that the bank keeps microfilmed copies and you can get duplicates in the event your records are misplaced or destroyed.

Frequent bank deposits get funds earning interest and reduce the chance of losing the cash or checks. But frequent deposits take more time. Making deposits twice a week works out well in most situations.

Remember. . . depositing Friday mornings will earn an extra 3 days interest versus depositing Friday afternoons.

To ensure proper crediting of your deposits, write or stamp "For Deposit Only to Account #" on the back of each check. Many banks will supply you a personalized stamp free of charge.

A good place to hold duplicate deposit slips and negotiable checks is in the plastic envelope provided in most 3-Up check binders.

eg Our business activities begin with an owner contribution of $500, and a bank loan of $500. The deposit slip is completed as shown in Figure 2. Note that the income category NON-TAXABLE is entered on the top of the slip.

FIGURE 2 The Deposit Slip

We price our book at $10.00 which will include postage and handling. Product sales in our state are subject to a 5% sales tax, bringing the total sales price to $10.50 for sales made within the state. Payment will be required in advance to save the costs of billing and collecting for such small sales.

Figure 3 shows our deposit of our book sale income. Note that we have listed each check individually so that the deposit slips can also serve as a record of when and to whom books were sold (which would help resolve any future questions). The deposit is labeled PRODUCTS, indicating the income is from product sales which are subject to taxes in our state.

Product sales exempt from state sales tax are entered on a separate deposit slip labeled PRODUCTS, NO SALES TAX. the two-letter state abbreviation is noted after purchaser's name for out-of-state sales; US for sales to US government; NP for non-profit exemption.

We price our consulting services at $50/hr with a two hour minimum. Since it's customary to pay for services _after_ the work is completed, we need a way to keep track of who purchased the services, who has paid and who owes money. See Appendix b for description of a simple and efficient billing system.

Income from sales of services is handled in the same manner as other deposits. When money is received, the purchaser and amount are recorded on a deposit slip marked SERVICES and deposited. These services are currently not subject to sales tax in our state.

At the end of our first month (January), we have a total of 5 deposit slips, 3 slips for Product sales totaling $220.50, 1 slip for Services totaling: $250.00; and 1 Non-Taxable income slip totaling: $1000.00 (Figure 4).

DATE 1-18 19 91	DOLLARS	CENTS
CURRENCY		
COINS		
CHECKS		
1 G. SWEAZY	10	50
2 J. BINSTED	10	50
3 A. USTIN	10	50
4 R. LITTLE	10	50
5 P. BRYANT	10	50
TOTAL DEPOSIT	52	50

FIGURE 3 Deposit Showing Individual Sales

9

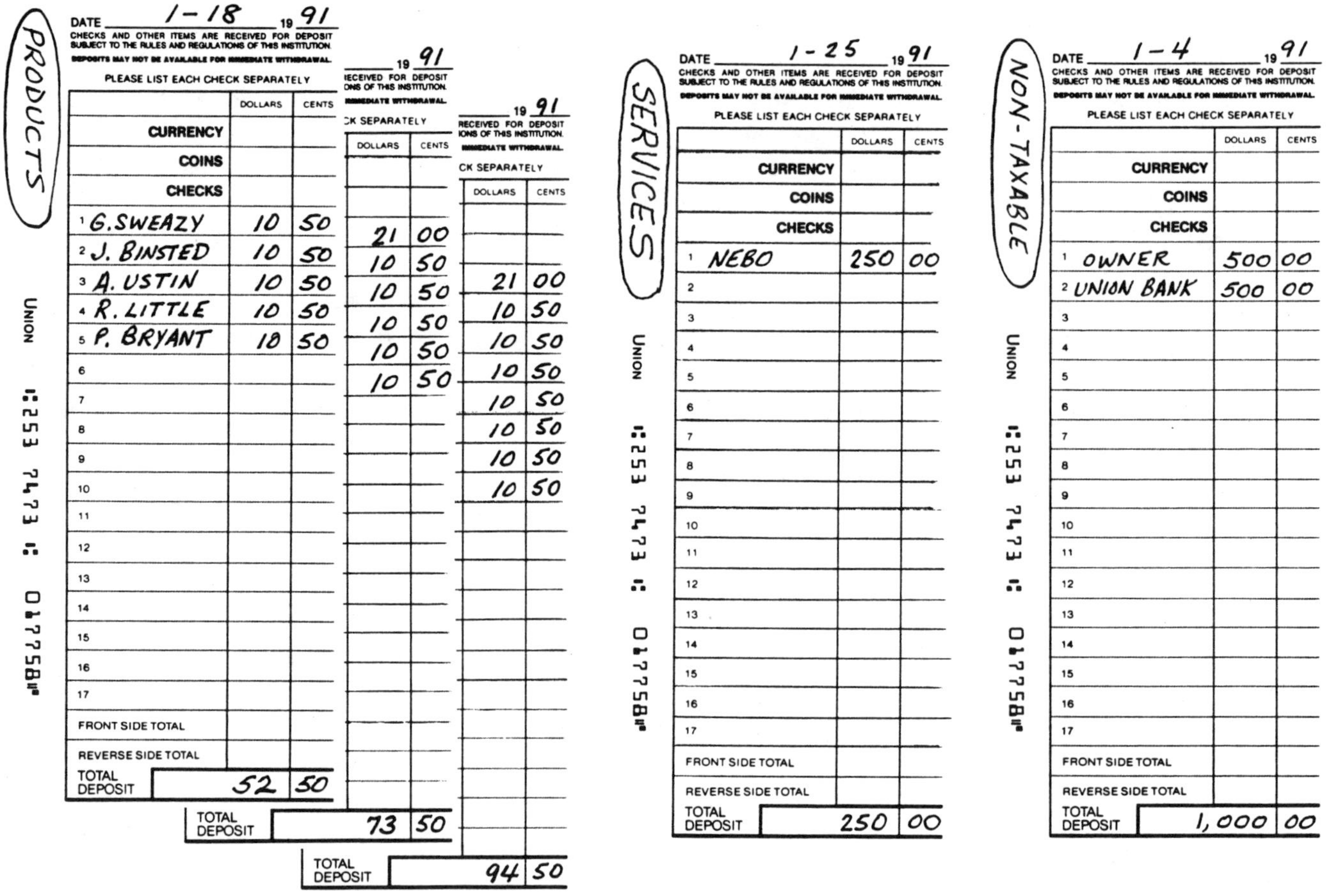

FIGURE 4 Grouping Deposit Slips By Income Category

Note that our deposit slips show sales including sales tax ($220.50). Recording the total in this way is very efficient, but it's important to know how much of the total figure is sales tax. To find out, we do the following calculation:

1. *Add 1.00 to the decimal tax rate (our tax rate of 5% expressed as a decimal is .05, adding 1.00 = 1.05).*

2. *Divide figure from (1) above into the total collected to get the Product total (220.50 - 1.05 = 210.00).*

3. *Subtract Product total from total amount collected to find the Sales Tax total (220.50 - 210.00 = 10.50).*

CHECK: Product total + Sales Tax = Total collected ($210.00 + $10.50 = $220.50).

This simple calculation saves time and paperwork in not having to record the sales tax on each sale, then totalling long lists of product and tax income.

10

Our total income for each category is entered on the appropriate line of the Financial Summary (Figure 5). That done, the deposit slips and the paid invoice are filed in a large manila envelope marked, "January 1991."

Category	JAN			QTR	YTD
Begin Balance					
PRODUCTS	210.00				
SERVICES	250.00				
INTEREST					
MISCL					
SALES TAX	10.50				
NON-TAX	1,000.00				
INCOME					

FINANCIAL SUMMARY '91

FIGURE 5 Financial Summary Showing Income

11

chapter 3

money going out

What Are The Two Major Types Of Business Expenses?

There are two major types of business spending: operating and capital expenditures. Operating expenses are those needed to keep the business going day to day, such as auto fuel or office supplies. Capital expenses are purchases that will serve the business for a number of years, such as the automobile or the office equipment. Not surprisingly, the two are treated differently for tax purposes; operating expenses are fully tax deductible in the year the purchases are made,

whereas deductions for capital expenditures must usually be pro-rated over the property's useful life.

How Many Categories Are Needed To Track Expenses?

There are more ways for money to leave a business than to enter it, so more categories are required to track expenses. The number of categories needed ranges from about a dozen for the typical sideline business, to nearly twice that for a business involving employees, products and services. The Financial Summary provides space for 22 categories.

What Are The Common Operating Expense Categories?

Merchandise & Material	Travel
Advertising	Meals/Entertainment
Telephone	Dues/Publications
Office Supplies	Refunds
Rents	State & Local Taxes
Utilities	Bank Charges
Repairs & Maintenance	Wages
Insurance	Payroll Taxes
Interest	Employee Benefits
Contract Services	Miscellaneous
Car/Truck	Non-Deductible

A definition for each expense category is provided in the Appendix c. Naturally, you may use these categories and definitions or combine and change them to suit your needs.

Where Are Capital Equipment Expenses Entered?

Since the deductibility of capital expenses are subject to IRS restrictions and determined at the end of the year, such expenses are entered as *Non-Deductible*. The appropriate deduction is calculated and entered as part of the year-end routine (Chapter 4).

What Expenses Are Not Deductible?

Just as owner contributions and loans are not taxable income, *owner withdrawals* and *repayments of loan principal* are not tax deductible and are entered in this category. It's important to note that the interest paid on the loan is deductible. When the amount of principal and interest are known, the interest portion is entered as Interest and the principal portion as Non-Deductible. Otherwise, the entire payment may be entered as Non-Deductible, and adjusted at the end of the year upon receipt of the statement showing the amount of interest paid.

How Do Check Duplicates & Receipts Serve As Records?

Since nearly all business expenses will be paid by check, the duplicate copies made as the checks are written - together with receipts for unavoidable cash purchases - comprise the expense record.

By noting the expense category on the line provided on the lower left side of each check, and noting the expense category on each cash receipt, expenses can be totaled by category each month (see Figure 6). Category totals are transferred to the Financial Summary, and the check duplicates and receipts are filed away. The bank's microfilmed check records provide a valuable back-up in the event original records are lost or destroyed.

How Do You Avoid Getting Buried In Paper?

The secret to keeping up with all the bits and pieces of paper is to collect all such papers in an accordion folder (Figure 7) and sort it out at the end of the month as follows:

1. Group all bills together and then divide into paid and unpaid.

2. Write checks for unpaid bills noting expense category on the check. Write "paid" and the date on each bill to prevent

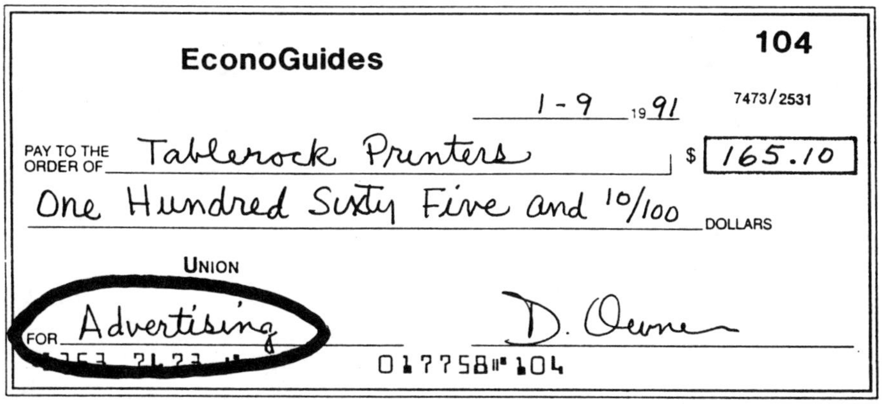

FIGURE 6 Check Noting Expense Category

duplicating payment in future. Staple all paid bills together.

3. Group cash receipts, credit card slips, and business phone calls and other outlays made on behalf of the business. Total and write a check for this amount to reimburse yourself for such out-of-pocket expenses. Be sure to note "reimbursement cash expenses" on check.

4. Group the duplicate copies of checks written during month and separate them into expense categories (do not include the check to reimburse yourself in the groupings. Since this check usually covers expenses from several categories, we exclude it and use the individual cash receipts instead—see step 5.

5. Distribute the cash receipts gathered in step 3 to the appropriate expense category, then total the checks and cash receipts in each category using an adding machine. Staple checks and cash receipts together; adding machine tape with category name should be on top.

6. Check math: The total amount of all categories should equal total amount of all checks written during the month (including the one reimbursing yourself). If totals don't match, find and correct the error. When totals agree, transfer each category total to the Financial Summary.

7. Place stapled bundles of paid bills, checks and receipts into the 9"x12" the manila envelope marked with month and year.

Make sure you have some supporting piece of paper, like a bill or receipt, before writing a check or spending cash. Anyone who has been audited knows that a canceled check by itself is not proof of a necessary business expense. In the absence of such supporting paper, simply make your own note of the business purpose served by the expense.

It's best to officially start your business *before* you pay *any* business related expenses such as research, travel, legal or other setup costs. The reason is that the expenses which *precede* the establishment of the business may be considered "organization" costs which are not fully deductible in the year spent but must be spread over a 5 year period.

In January, we wrote eleven checks; ten for purchases and one reimbursing the owner for the following expenses:

$40.75   Business phone calls (underlined on the residential phone bill)
43.40   Gas & oil (credit cards slips)
36.75   Business dinner (credit card slip with business purpose noted)
2.00   Pocket calendar (cash receipt)
$ 122.90   TOTAL

The check duplicates and cash receipts were grouped and totaled by expense category (Figure 8). Since the total of all these category figures ($1153.00) is the same as the total of all the checks written during the month—including the check reimbursing owner for cash expenses —the category figures can be transferred to the Financial Summary (Figure 9).

FIGURE 7 Folder for Current Expenses

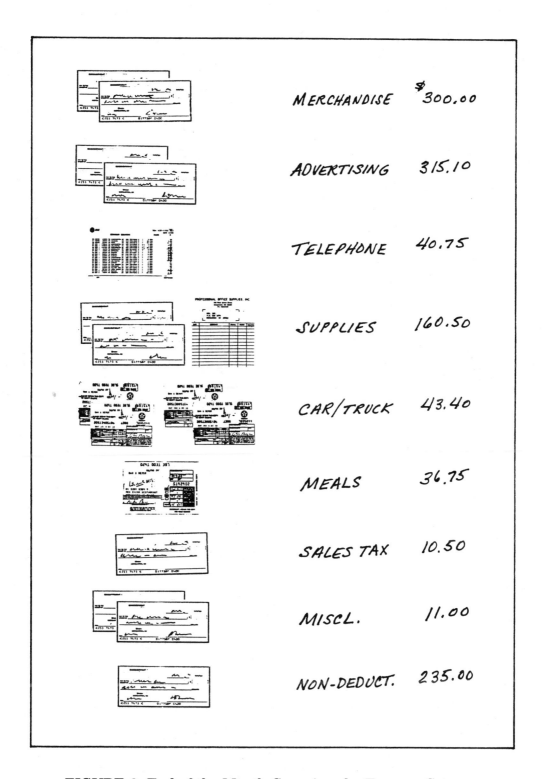

MERCHANDISE	$300.00
ADVERTISING	315.10
TELEPHONE	40.75
SUPPLIES	160.50
CAR/TRUCK	43.40
MEALS	36.75
SALES TAX	10.50
MISCL.	11.00
NON-DEDUCT.	235.00

FIGURE 8 End of the Month Groupings by Expense Category

17

FINANCIAL SUMMARY '91					
Category	JAN			QTR	YTD
Begin Balance					
INCOME					
MERCHDSE	300.00				
ADVERTISE	315.10				
TELEPHONE	40.75				
OFFICE SUPP	160.50				
RENT					
MAINT/REP					
INSURANCE					
INTEREST					
CONTRACT					
CAR/TRUCK	43.40				
TRAVEL					
MEALS/ENT	36.75				
DUES/PUB					
REFUNDS					
SALES TAX	10.50				
BANK CHG					
MISCL	11.00				
NON-DED	235.00				
EXPENSE					
GAIN (LOSS)					
End Balance					

FIGURE 9 Financial Summary Showing Expenses

chapter 4

tally-ho! bottom line

When Are Bottom Lines Usually Calculated?

The bottom line is the final score of some financial event. Most businesses find it helpful as well as necessary to calculate their bottom lines:

- Monthly: to control paper clutter; assure books and bank statement agree.

- Quarterly: to compare and control budget and expenses; figure quarterly tax.

- Annually: to close books; figure federal and state income taxes.

What Calculations Are Made At The End Of Each Month?

At the close of each month, usually soon after the bank statement is received, the following calculations are made:

- Gain (or loss): total income less total expense.

- Book Balance: beginning balance plus Gain (or Loss).

- Bank Balance: adjust for outstanding checks & deposits.

- Proving Books: assure "book" and "bank" balances agree.

19

Exactly How Is The Monthly Gain Or Loss Figured?

1. Find the Total Income (#1, Figure 10) by:
   - Entering total for each Income category.
   - Entering Interest or credits from bank statement.
   - Totaling all Income categories.

2. Find Total Expenses (#2, Figure 10) by:
   - Entering total of each Expense category
   - Entering Bank Charges (bank statement)
   - Totaling all Expense categories

3. Find Monthly Gain or Loss (#3, Figure 10) by:
   - Subtracting Total Expense (2) from Income (1)
   - Showing any resulting (loss) in parenthesis.

Take a few moments to check the adding machine tape and make certain each figure is correctly entered; this precaution will save you time and frustration as most imbalances are traceable to such original entry errors.

What Is The Book Balance And How Is It Found?

The book balance is the ending balance shown on the company's books or financial records. Our book balance is literally the bottom line of the Financial Summary, and is simply the Gain (or Loss) added to the beginning balance (see #4 Figure 10). Note that the balance at the end of the month is entered as the beginning balance (top line) for the next month.

If a monthly loss is greater than the beginning balance, the resulting (negative) ending balance is shown in parenthesis.

How Do You Find The End Of Month Bank Balance?

The ending balance on your bank statement (Figure 11) *will usually be different* from the ending balance on your Financial Summary because some of the checks you've written have not yet cleared the bank, and/or some deposit(s) were made *after* the statement's closing date. The necessary adjustment, or reconciliation, is made on the reverse side of the Financial Summary (Figure 12).

The procedure is as follows:

1. Enter the ending balance shown on bank statement (may also be called new or current balance), then add any deposit(s) made during the month that are not shown on the statement.

2. List and total checks that are still outstanding; that is, not shown on statement(s).

3. Find end of month bank balance by subtracting (2) from (1) above; balance should agree with the ending balance on the reverse side.

20

Category	JAN	FEB		QTR	YTD
FINANCIAL SUMMARY '91					
Begin Balance	0.00	319.50			
PRODUCTS	210.00				
SERVICES	250.00				
INTEREST	2.00				
MISCL					
SALES TAX	10.50				
NON-TAX	1,000.00				
① INCOME	1,472.50				
MERCHDSE	300.00				
ADVERTISE	315.10				
TELEPHONE	40.75				
OFFICE SUPP	160.50				
RENT					
MAINT/REP					
INSURANCE					
INTEREST					
CONTRACT					
CAR/TRUCK	43.40				
TRAVEL					
MEALS/ENT	36.75				
DUES/PUB					
REFUNDS					
SALES TAX	10.50				
BANK CHG					
MISCL	11.00				
NON-DED	235.00				
② EXPENSE	1,153.00				
③ GAIN (LOSS)	319.50				
④ End Balance	319.50				

FIGURE 10 The Financial Summary - First Month

UNION BANK

ACCOUNT STATEMENT

Acct # 017758   Statement Date 01-25-91

Balance as of 01-25-91 $558.40

DEBITS

Check #	Date Posted	Amount
101	01-05	$ 6.00
102	01-09	$ 5.00
103	01-25	$ 235.00
104	01-20	$ 165.10
105	01-16	$ 150.00
106	01-19	$ 36.15
107	01-21	$ 122.35
*109	01-25	$ 100.00

*indicates break in sequence

SERVICE CHARGES

Minimum Balance Maintained   .00

DEPOSITS/CREDITS

Customer Deposit	01-05	$1000.00
Customer Deposit	01-18	$ 52.50
Customer Deposit	01-20	$ 73.50
Customer Deposit	01-25	$ 250.00
Interest Payment	01-25	$ 2.00

ACCOUNT SUMMARY

Beginning Balance	$ 0.00
Deposits	$1376.00
Interest Earned	$ 2.00
Debits	$ 819.60
Service Charges	$ 0.00
Ending Balance	$ 558.40

FIGURE 11 Monthly Bank Statement

BANK BALANCE						
MONTH	JANUARY					
STATEMENT BALANCE	DATE	AMOUNT	DATE	AMOUNT	DATE	AMOUNT
	1-25	558.40				
ADD DEPOSITS NOT SHOWN AND TOTAL 1. BELOW	1-28	94.50				
1.TOTAL DEPOSIT		652.90				
LIST ALL OUT-STANDING CHECKS AND TOTAL 2. BELOW	#108	200.00				
	#110	10.50				
	#111	122.90				
2. OUTSTANDING		333.40				
END BALANCE (2-1)		319.50				

FIGURE 12 Finding The End Of Month Bank Balance

Exactly How Do You Prove The Books?

Proving the books is simply assuring that the end of month book and bank balances are exactly the same. The Financial Summary makes verification easy by placing all the necessary data on the reverse sides of the same piece of paper.

If the balances are not the same, a mistake has been made and must be found and corrected. When balances agree, your books are proved and you may file away that month's financial papers.

You'll find a good way to minimize time, errors and frustration is by following the above routine as soon as *your bank statement arrives*. Also, if you pay your bills shortly after you receive your statement, most of the checks will clear before the next statement, reducing the number of outstanding checks and simplifying calculations. Make all entries and calculations in pencil so any mistakes are easily corrected. See Appendix d for hints on locating balance errors.

How Are The Month's Papers And Receipts Filed?

The Financial Summary is usually kept handy in a folder or loose leaf book and all the various supporting papers gathered during the month are filed away in a 9"x12" envelope marked with the month and year. This size envelope is large enough to hold a quantity of various sized papers yet fits neatly into a standard file or file storage box.

Each month's envelope will contain:

- bank statement and canceled checks,
- deposit slips (stapled by category),
- paid invoices (stapled in numerical order),
- duplicate checks & cash receipts (by category).

An exception to filing everything in the monthly envelope are receipts for the purchase of major equipment that is depreciated over several years. Such receipts should be kept in a folder labeled Equipment.

This filing system will enable you to quickly locate any financial backup document—even years later when audits are usually made. Being packaged by month and year, the stored files are easily rotated and discarded when no longer needed. The required retention period is a minimum of 3 years after the tax return is due; however, many experts advise records be kept 6 years, and longer if tax returns are complex and audit prone.

Why Are Quarterly Summaries Needed?

Quarterly summaries provide an excellent basis for reviewing and updating financial plans. A three month period is long enough to smooth out monthly fluctuations, yet short enough to correct negative trends before they become too serious.

Quarterly summaries also provide the figures needed for *quarterly tax reports* which the business may be required to file, such as:

- federal payroll & unemployment taxes
- state & local payroll taxes
- state unemployment tax
- estimated federal & state income taxes
- state and local sales taxes

How Is The Quarterly Summary Calculated?

At the end of each calendar quarter (March, June, September, and December), the category totals for the three month period are totaled and cross-checked (Figure 13). Here's the procedure:

1. Add each income category figure <u>across</u> and enter total at right. Cross-check these total figures by adding the quarter total column figures <u>down</u>. The Total Income (#1 Figure 13) should equal the monthly totals added <u>across</u> ($3014.25). If totals don't agree, check adding machine tape for entry error.

2. Add each expense category figure <u>across</u> and enter total at right. Cross-check these totals by adding the total quarter column figures <u>down</u>. The total quarter expense (#2 Figure 13) should equal the monthly totals added <u>across</u> ($2654.25); If the totals don't agree, check tape for entry error.

3. The gain or loss for the quarter (#3, Figure 13) is the total expense (#2) subtracted from total income (#1). The total should equal the sum of the monthly gains (or losses) added <u>across</u> ($360.00); if totals do not agree, check tape.

4. The ending quarter balance (#4, Figure 13) is the quarter gain or loss (#3) added to the beginning balance of the quarter. The result should be the same as the ending balance of last month in the quarter (#360.00); if not, find and correct the error. Unlike other quarter totals, the beginning and ending balance will <u>not</u> be the sum of the monthly balances added across.

The reason that first quarter totals are entered in the YTD (Year-To-Date) instead of the QTR (quarter) column is two-fold: first quarter totals <u>are</u> the year-to-date totals; and using the YTD column makes it easier to add second quarter figures.

Figure 14 illustrates how the quarterly reports can be positioned to compute the YTD totals without recopying figures. For illustration purposes all four quarters are shown, but in practice only two sheets are used at any one time. Similarly, only the total lines have been shown to simplify understanding. For example, note how first quarter income total of $3014.25 is aligned with and easily added to second quarter income total of $4733.25 to get the second quarter YTD total of $7747.50. The YTD totals are obtained for each category in the same manner.

FINANCIAL SUMMARY '91					
Category	JAN	FEB	MAR	QTR	YTD
Begin Balance	0.00	319.50	728.55		0.00
PRODUCTS	210.00	320.00	430.00		960.00
SERVICES	250.00	350.00	400.00		1,000.00
INTEREST	2.00	2.15	2.10		6.25
MISCL					
SALES TAX	10.50	16.00	21.50		48.00
NON-TAX	1,000.00				1,000.00
INCOME	1,472.50	688.15	853.60		3,014.25 ①
MERCHDSE	300.00		300.00		600.00
ADVERTISE	315.10		390.00		705.10
TELEPHONE	40.75	46.20	56.75		143.70
OFFICE SUPP	160.50	40.85	227.10		428.45
RENT					
MAINT/REP			14.90		14.90
INSURANCE					
INTEREST			15.00		15.00
CONTRACT		36.00	85.00		121.00
CAR/TRUCK	43.40	46.45	43.10		132.95
TRAVEL					
MEALS/ENT	36.75	39.60	56.50		132.85
DUES/PUB		40.35			40.35
REFUNDS		10.50			10.50
SALES TAX	10.50	16.00	21.50		48.00
BANK CHG			10.00		10.00
MISCL	11.00	3.15	2.30		16.45
NON-DED	235.00				235.00
EXPENSE	1,153.00	279.10	1,222.15		2,654.25 ②
GAIN (LOSS)	319.50	409.05	<368.55>		360.00 ③
End Balance	319.50	728.55	360.00		360.00 ④

FIGURE 13 First Quarter Financial Summary

eg *Our Financial Summary (Figure 13) indicates that:*

In February
- *we paid $36.00 for Contract Services (temporary secretarial help)*
- *we paid $10.50 for Refund (to a book customer)*

In March
- *we paid $227.10 for office supplies. (This total included $175 for a used copy machine which, being less that $200, doesn't have to be depreciated)*
- *we paid $15.00 Interest (on $500 bank loan)*
- *a $10.00 bank charge appeared on the Bank Statement.*

Since the total Expense was more than the total Income during the month, the resulting loss of $368.55 is indicated placing figure in parenthesis.

The bank was notified their $10 charge was in error and they said our account would be credited on the next statement. We will show that $10 credit as Misc. Income on our Financial Statement.

How Are The Year-End Figures Determined?

Since the quarterly summaries provide year-to-date totals, the YTD column of the fourth quarter <u>is</u> the year-end summary of all cash that came into, went out of, and remains in the business, including any reimbursement to owner for business use of the home.

However, since these cash flow totals include non-taxable income and non-deductible expenses, some adjustments must be made before the figures can be entered on tax returns.

How Is The Year's *Taxable* Gain (Profit) Determined?

For *Cash Method* businesses which don't involve sales from inventory, figures from the fourth quarter YTD column may be copied to the Taxable column of the Annual Summary (Figure 15) rounding each figure to the nearest dollar.

Since Sales Taxes collected and Loans are not taxable income, these sums are excluded from the Taxable column. Similarly, Sales Taxes paid are not deductible, and are excluded from the Taxable column.

Meals and Entertainment expenses, are currently only 80% deductible—so this total is reduced by 20%.

Lastly, allowable Depreciation is calculated and entered as an expense (see next chapter for explanation of depreciation expenses).

Accrual Method businesses whose income involves sales from inventory, must make all of the above adjustments *plus* the following (which bring books to accrual):

1. Add to the appropriate income category the dollar value of *accounts receivable* as of December 31.

2. Add to appropriate expense category the dollar value of *unpaid bills* as of December 31.

3. Adjust income to reflect the dollar value of *inventory* on hand as of December 31. (The cost of unsold goods is not deductible).

Category	JAN	FEB	MAR	1 QTR	YTD	2 QTR '91	YTD	3 QTR '91	YTD	4 QTR '91	YTD
Begin Balance	0.00	319.50	728.55		0.00	360.00	0.00	2,090.10	0.00	4,153.35	0.00
PRODUCTS	210.00	320.00	430.00		960.00						
SERVICES	250.00	350.00	400.00		1,000.00						
INTEREST	2.00	2.15	2.10		6.25						
MISCL											
SALES TAX	10.50	16.00	21.50		48.00						
NON-TAX	1,000.00				1,000.00						
INCOME	1,472.50	688.15	853.60		3,014.25	4,733.25	7,747.50	5,110.75	12,858.25	6,324.75	19,183.00
MERCHDSE	300.00		300.00		600.00						
ADVERTISE	315.10		390.00		705.10						
TELEPHONE	40.75	46.20	56.75		143.70						
OFFICE SUPP	160.50	40.85	227.10		428.45						
RENT											
MAINT/REP			14.90		14.90						
INSURANCE											
INTEREST		15.00			15.00						
CONTRACT		36.00	85.00		121.00						
CAR/TRUCK	43.40	46.45	43.10		132.95						
TRAVEL											
MEALS/ENT	36.75	39.60	56.50		132.85						
DUES/PUB		40.35			40.35						
REFUNDS		10.50			10.50						
SALES TAX	10.50	16.00	21.50		48.00						
BANK CHG		10.00			10.00						
MISCL	11.00	3.15	2.30		16.45						
NON-DED	235.00				235.00						
EXPENSE	1,153.00	279.10	1,222.15		2,654.25	3,003.15	5,657.40	3,047.50	8,704.90	7,048.10	15,753.00
GAIN (LOSS)	319.50	409.05	<368.55>		360.00	1,730.10	2,090.10	2,063.25	4,153.35	723.35	3,430.00
End Balance	319.50	728.55	360.00		360.00	2,090.10	2,090.10	4,153.35	4,153.35	3,430.00	3,430.00

FINANCIAL SUMMARY '91

FIGURE 14 Positioning Quarterly Summaries For YTD Totaling

28

199_ ANNUAL SUMMARY			
CATEGORY	YTD	ADJ	TAXABLE
Begin Balance	0.00		.
PRODUCTS	10,860.00		10,860
SERVICES	6,600.00	+600	7,200
INTEREST	138.50		139
MISCL	41.00		41
INVENTORY		+340	340
SALES TAX	543.50		
NON-TAX	1,000.00		
INCOME	19,183.00		18,580
MERCHDSE	3,000.00	+600	3,600
ADVERTISE	2,108.20	+200	2,308
TELEPHONE	682.25		682
OFFICE SUPP	924.20		924
RENT	1,849.00		1,849
MAINT/REP	47.50		48
INSURANCE	120.00		120
INTEREST	180.00		180
CONTRACT	690.00		690
CAR/TRUCK	1,343.50		1,344
TRAVEL	568.00		568
MEALS/ENT	674.60	−135	540
DUES/PUB	348.00		348
REFUNDS	63.00		63
SALES TAX	543.50		
BANK CHG	42.00		42
MISCL	99.25		99
WAGES	401.00	+79	480
PAYROLL TAX	134.00	−79	55
DEPRECIATION			3,635
NON-DED	1,935.00		
EXPENSE	15,753.00		17,575
GAIN (LOSS)	3,430.00		1,005
End Balance	3,430.00		

FIGURE 15   Annual Summary Showing Year's Taxable Gain

Why Must Year-End Receivables & Payables Be Flagged?

The year-end accrual adjustments have accounted for sums *not yet* received or spent. To prevent duplicating entries when these sums are *actually* received and paid out, we flag those receivables and payables by writing Receivable 1991 across the outstanding invoices, and Payable 1991 across the unpaid bills. So, in early 1992, when payment arrives for an invoice flagged Receivable 1991 you know this money has already been *accounted for and taxed* and should be deposited and recorded as Non-Taxable income. Similarly, in early 1992, when you pay a bill flagged payable 1991, you know this expense has already been deducted and your check and the Financial Summary should show this expense as Non-Deductible.

Which Balances Are Carried Forward Year-To-Year?

In addition to the ending book and bank balances, which are the bottom lines on the Annual Summary YTD column (Figure 15), other balances which must be recorded for use the following year are: Inventory; Equipment Cost and Loans. These balances are entered in the space provided on the reverse side of the Annual Summary (Figure 16).

eg *The Company's year-end balances and adjustments (Figure 15) were as follows:*

■ *Accounts Receivable* (on clipboard)
Two Invoices for Services
@ $300 each $600.00

■ *Bills Payable* (in expense envelope)
Merchandise $600.00
Advertising $200.00

■ *Inventory* (in store room)
Ending Value $340.00
Beginning Value $ 0.00

Adjustment* $340.00

* The inventory adjustment is: Ending Value minus Beginning Value. Note that it is positive in this case, but whenever the ending value is less than the beginning value the adjustment will be negative.

■ *Rent* - *The owner is allowed a deduction of $1849 for the business use of the home. A company check is written December 31 to reimburse the owner for this Rent expense (see next chapter for calculations).*

■ *Meals & Entertainment* - *The adjustment in the Meals and Entertainment figure reflects the current tax law limiting the deductibility to 80% of the total spent. The $135 reduction is 20% of $675 that is not deductible.*

■ *Gross Wages & Employer Payroll Taxes* - *The employee payroll record indicates gross wages were $480 which means $79 of the payroll tax category was employee taxes and the remaining ($55) was employer taxes.*

■ *Depreciation* - *The total equipment expense during the year was $5,235 (see Figure 16). Allowable depreciation was $3,635 (see next chapter for depreciation calculations).*

■ **The Year's Taxable Gain (Profit)** - The company's taxable gain for the year is $1,005, and is the total taxable income less total deductible expense (Figure 15).

1991 ANNUAL SUMMARY (Cont.)			
ASSET	COST	PAID	CREDIT
OFFICE EQUIP	235	235	0
TRUCK	4,000	400	3,600
COMPUTER	1,000	200	800
TOTAL ASSETS	5,235	835	4,400
CREDITOR	LOAN AMOUNT	REPAID PRINCIPAL	BALANCE
UNION BANK	500	500	0
CREDIT UNION	3,600	600	3,000
MT. MICRO	800	0	800
TOTAL LIABILITY	4,900	1,100	3,800
OWNER	Contributions 500	Withdrawals 0	Balance 500
INVENTORY VALUE	Beginning 0	Purchased 3,600	Ending 340

FIGURE 16 Ending Balances On Reverse Side of Annual Summary

chapter 5

fearless filing

What is Fearless Filing?

Fearless filing is taking full advantage of tax saving strategies without ever fearing a tax audit. Many happy returns are possible because your financial management system:

- embodies tax-wise planning
- internally checks all figures for accuracy
- provides documentation for each entry

How Is Business Profit Or Loss Reported?

A Sole Proprietorship reports profit/loss on Schedule C which is attached to the personal tax return form 1040 (see Appendix f for copy and explanation of a completed Schedule C).

What Is The Self Employment Tax?

The Self Employment Tax provides funds for Social Security and Medicare benefits for the self employed. The Tax is based on the profit figure shown on Schedule C. The tax is computed on Schedule SE and attached to the personal return. For 1991, the tax works out to just over 14%, but because one-half the tax is deductible the effective rate for most payers is just over 12% (see Appendix f for completed Schedule SE and 1040 forms).

For high wage earners, the good news is that the tax is capped at *combined* wage and self employment income ($53,400 for 1991).

Above that level, the tax drops to about 2.7% of earnings; and with half deductible, the effective rate for most payers is 2.3%. So a proprietor who earns over $53,400 in outside wages, would have business profits taxed at only 2.3%; a proprietor earning $43,400 in wages would be taxed 2.3% on business profits over $10,000, and so on. There is no self employment tax on income above combined wage and self employment earnings of $125,000 in 1991. For lower wage earners, the good news is that they may recover much of their self employment taxes through higher social security benefits than their wages alone would provide.

When Are Estimated Quarterly Tax Payments Required?

The rules say that a tax payer must make advanced quarterly payments if the tax due in the preceding year exceeded the amount withheld by more than $500. The payer will be subject to a penalty in the coming year if the amount withheld and estimated payments do not total 90% of the tax due that year. There is an important exception to this rule; if the total withheld and paid is at least equal to the previous year's tax, there is no penalty. Many sideline business owners take advantage of this exception by making sure the amounts withheld from their wages will total their previous year's tax. As the sideline business grows and the required payments become too large to be withheld from regular wages, owners pay the *difference* in four equal quarterly payments during the year. This approach enables the owner of a growing business to pay the least amount of estimated taxes without incurring a penalty.

(Note): Beginning in 1992, the no penalty exception described above will not apply to those with taxable incomes of over $75,000 when such income is more than $45,000 greater than the previous year.

What Are the Principal Tax Saving Strategies?

The major tax saving strategies arise from the business owner's ability to:

- control income
- depreciate and expense equipment
- deduct business use of home
- deduct business use of car
- deduct education and training costs
- deduct portion of health insurance premiums
- defer income by retirement contributions
- hire family members
- control inventory
- deduct travel, meals & entertainment expenses

How Can Owners Control Income?

Business owners can *reduce* taxable income by year-end moves delaying billing for goods or services sold, and speeding up planned purchases. Or, the owner can *increase* taxable income by speeding up billings and delaying purchases which is advisable when the owner expects the tax rates will be higher in the following year.

eg *The proprietor's income from wages and interest was nearly $40,000, a level at which adding several thousand dollars in business profits would result in reducing deductible IRA contributions and increase the tax effective tax rate from 15% to the 28% thereby wiping out much of the business profit.*

34

Recognizing that with the accrual method billing is the same as receiving and ordering is the same as paying, the owner was able to reduce business income a total of $2,300 by:

Delaying until January 1992 billing for $500 of consulting work done in December.

Accelerating planned purchases: computer ($1,000) merchandise ($600) and mailing labels ($200).

How Is Depreciation Calculated?

The tax rules say that the cost of equipment whose useful life is more than one year must be spread over the useful life. The cost includes purchase price, taxes, freight, and installation charges; it does not include finance charges which are deductible as interest in the year paid. If you think the property will be worth more than 10% of its original cost at the end of its useful life, you must deduct the estimated salvage value from the cost. The useful life is determined by the IRS; for example, autos, light trucks, computers, and office equipment are classed as 5-year property, whereas office furniture and fixtures are classed as 7-year property.

There are two ways to calculate depreciation: *straight line* and *declining balance*. In the *straight line* method, the total purchase price is divided by its useful life and the amount of depreciation is the same each year. In the *declining balance* method, the depreciation is greater in the early years; you have a choice of 200% or 150% declining rates, the former allowing a little faster depreciation. If the straight line method is chosen, it must be used for the entire life of the property. If the declining balance method is chosen you may change to straight line at the point it results in a higher deduction.

The straight line method works out better if business is growing, or tax rates are rising. Also, using the straight line method prevents the "recapture" of excess deductions if you dispose of the property before its useful life ends or if business use falls below 50%.

With either method, the amount of first year depreciation is limited by the "half year" or "mid quarter" rules. These rules say that regardless of the date of purchase, all property, except real estate, is assumed to have been placed into service at the mid-point of the year reducing the allowable first year depreciation by half. If more than 40% of all property acquired during the year is purchased in the last 3 months of the year, then the more limited "mid-quarter" rules apply; to maximize depreciation, try to make major purchases before October.

Real estate purchases use a "mid-month" rule; cars and light trucks are subject to special annual depreciation limits. Naturally, if use of the property will be partly business and partly personal, the depreciation expense is limited to the business use portion.

Keep in mind that you can depreciate property or equipment you owned prior to going into business using purchase price or fair market value (whichever is lower) as the cost basis.

What Is The First Year *Expensing* Deduction?

First year Expensing is a special provision

of the tax code (Section 179) which allows deducting up to $10,000 of the cost of certain business equipment the year it is placed in service. The deduction is subject to the following limitations:

The property must be used more than 50% in the *active* conduct of business, and the deduction is limited to business use portion.

The deduction is limited to business profits *excluding the cost of the property*. That means if the business made only $5,000 profit that year, only $5,000 worth of equipment may be Expensed that year—but the remaining $5,000 can be carried over to the following year making the Section 179 limit $15,000 rather than $10,000.

The deduction reduces the depreciation basis of the property. That means if the equipment costs $10,000 and a Section 179 deduction of $5,000 is taken, depreciation is figured on the remaining amount—$5,000—not the original $10,000 cost. Deduction is subject to pay back (recapture) on future returns if business use falls below 50% or the property is disposed of before it is fully depreciated.

Passenger cars and light trucks are subject a special limit; the total first year deduction for depreciation *and* Expensing cannot exceed $2660 in 1991.

The deduction is not allowed for buildings, furnishings or personal property you already own and are converting to business use.

If you need a deduction and are short the cash, consider purchasing needed equipment on an installments and Expensing the total cost under the Section 179 deduction. Installment purchases are treated as if the entire price is paid when the purchase agreement is signed. However, be aware that using accelerated depreciation methods, may make you liable to AMT or the Alternative Minimum Tax. For instance, this can happen when depreciation and certain other deductions added back to the taxable income of joint filers exceed $40,000; if the excess amount multiplied by 24% is greater than the tax figured the regular way, they would have to pay the higher amount. Faced with such a situation, you could forgo the expensing option in order to reduce the amount of depreciation taken.

The equipment purchased and total depreciation taken for the first year is shown below (see Appendix e for calculations).

ITEM	COST	1ST YR DEPRECIATION
Furniture	$ 235	$ 235
Truck	4000	2400
Computer	1000	1000
Total	$5235	$3635

What Is The Deduction For Business Use Of The Home?

If a portion of your home is used exclusively for business, you are permitted a deduction for expenses related to that portion. The rules say that the deduction *cannot exceed the net income from the business*, but you can carry any disallowed expense forward for use in a later year. The allowable deduction is computed on Form 8829 and attached to the personal return.

If you are planning to sell your home in the near future, claiming the business use deduction may not be wise; instead of being able to defer taxes on the entire gain from the sale by purchasing another home of similar or greater value within 2 years, you would be subject to immediate taxes on the portion being claimed for business use - 15% of the total gain in the above case. This could wipe out the benefits from the business use deduction, and then some, if your home has appreciated a lot. Currently, you can avoid the tax if you haven't claimed the deduction in the year prior to the sale. But regulations change, so consult a preparer if there's a possibility you'll be selling your home.

Although mortgage interest and property taxes are itemized deductions, many owners can benefit from taking the deductions against business income because it reduces the self-employment tax. However, for high wage earners who are already paying the maximum Social Security taxes, it is better to take these as itemized deductions in order to maximize the amount they can shelter through their business retirement plan.

Don't forget that expenses to fix-up, decorate, furnish and clean the home office are also deductible. And you don't have to buy new things; you can convert some of your personal furnishings to business use and depreciate them also as long as you can document how much the items cost.

Most homeowner policies exclude or limit coverage for business assets and liability. However, for a nominal cost you can add a "rider" to cover business assets and increase your liability limits by purchasing an "umbrella" liability policy.

The owner's home is 2000 sq. ft; the office space, including storage area, is 300 sq. ft. Therefore, the business use portion is 15% of all applicable housing expenses:

mortgage interest
real estate taxes
insurance
maintenance & repairs
utilities
other misc. expenses
depreciation

The deduction for business use of the owner's home is $1849. Since the net income from the business before applying the business use deduction is greater ($2854), the entire $1849 is deductible this year (see Appendix f for calculations on form 8829).

How Is The Business Use Of Personal Auto Deducted?

Business owners who use their personal auto for business have a choice of either deducting the actual operating cost or the IRS mileage allowance (27.5 cents per business mile in 1991). Actual operating costs include depreciation, insurance, state and local taxes, fuel, maintenance and repair - multiplied by the percentage of business use. The percentage of business use is simply the number of business miles divided by the total number of miles driven during the year.

The choice of actual cost or flat rate must be made the first year the auto is placed in service; if actual cost is chosen, you may not switch to the flat rate for that vehicle in any later year.

The Actual Cost method usually works out better for higher value autos, while the flat rate, which is subject to change each year, is usually better for older, less expensive autos. Regardless of the method chosen, you will need to record the odometer reading at the beginning and end of each year, and record each business trip in order to support the deduction claimed.

Business and total mileage figures on personal autos used in business must be reported on Form 4562 attached to the personal return.

eg *A total of 2,925 business miles were placed on the owner's personal car. As the operating costs on this auto are low and business use represented only 24% of the total miles driven during the year, the mileage allowance deduction was chosen (2,925 x .275 = $804). Since the owner, had been reimbursed $232 for fuel and other operating expenses during the year, a check for $572 (804-232 = 572) was issued to the owner in December and included in the car/truck category that month on the Financial Summary. See Appendix f for completed Form 4562 reporting mileage on autos used in business.*

What Educational Expenses Are Deductible?

The tax rules provide for deductions for any education expenses that enable you to keep up with your field or which will help further your business. Allowable educational expenses include dues and subscriptions, tuition and materials, and travel to seminars and workshops. You cannot deduct education costs that prepare you for a new profession.

Note that while these educational expenses might also qualify as a miscellaneous deduction on the personal return, these deductions must exceed, and are reduced by 2% of the adjusted gross income for most taxpayers. The business owner benefits from full deduction of educational costs as well as greatly expanding the areas of legitimate study and training in pursuit of business goals.

eg *During the year, the owner subscribed to, and was reimbursed for, a number of trade and business publications and the books and tuition for a college course and weekend workshop.*

What Are Travel, Meals & Entertainment Deductions?

Travel, meals, and entertainment expenses which are undertaken primarily to further the business are deductible expenses. However, meals and entertainment expenses are only 80% deductible and this reduction is made as a year-end adjustment.

Travel and entertainment expenses get close attention by the IRS. You avoid any questions by noting on the travel and entertainment receipts the name and business purpose and relationship of any guest. For example, you might write on the credit card receipt, or meal stub, "B. Baruch, business associate, re: financing expansion."

The hotel receipt, or piece of hotel stationery, is a handy place to jot down cash outlays for tips to porters at the airport and hotel, parking, tolls, taxi fares, phone calls, coffee, shoe shines, and other incidentals. Some experienced travelers use a diary to record such expenses. This works well if the diary also serves other purposes, and if you don't lose it. Otherwise, you could save money and worry by simply getting in the habit of noting cash expenses as mentioned. Cash outlays of over $25 should be supported by a receipt. Keep copies of convention and seminar programs to support business relationship.

eg The owner was reimbursed for the full cost of attending a business seminar in a distant city where the owner could entertain and freely discuss business matters with knowledgeable persons who were not direct competitors. Note that the traveller is reimbursed the full cost of meals and entertainment; it's the deduction that's limited to 80% of costs.

What Are The Benefits Of Hiring Family Members?

Children under 18 employed in the family business are exempt from social security and unemployment taxes, which reduces the costs to the business for such help. Since each individual is entitled to a standard deduction, the first $3,400 earned in 1991 is tax free; while earnings between $3,400 and $20,350 are taxed at only 15%. But perhaps the best part is that parents can continue to claim their children as exemptions on their personal returns until the youngsters are 19 years old (or under 24 if full-time student) provided the child earned less than $2,150 in 1991 and the parents provided half of their support.

If the spouse is employed in the business, the wages are subject to Social Security, Medicare and Income taxes, but not federal unemployment tax. However, the spouse may contribute to the business's retirement plan (and also a deductible IRA if the family's adjusted gross income is under $50,000).

The advantages of hiring family members are that it keeps the money in the family, it reduces the overall taxes paid, and it doesn't increase your legal liability. As long as the wages paid to family members are reasonable for the work being done, you need not worry about any questions or challenges from the IRS.

The major drawback to hiring a family member, or anyone else, is that it triggers an avalanche of paperwork. And this unending flow of federal and state reports begins as soon as you put on even one, part-time employee.

Hiring family members can also complicate and strain family relationships because business problems are carried over to family life and visa-versa. Unless you're prepared for and able to manage such strains it may be wise to keep family and business dealings separate.

There is no lower age limit for hiring children in a family's unincorporated business, but work and wages must match the youngster's capabilities (see Appendix h for additional hints on becoming an employer).

eg In December, the owner's 18 year old daughter was hired to do clerical work 20 hours per week @ $6.00/hour ($480/month). Because she is over 18, her wages are subject to Social Security and Medicare taxes (see Appendix h, for explanation of employment taxes and records).

How Is Income Deferred Through A Retirement Plan?

Potentially the most important tax deduction available to the self-employed is the retirement plan contribution. For sole proprietors, this deduction is taken as an adjustment to Income (line 27) on the 1040 form. The deduction is critical to reducing income taxes when business profits become sizeable. However, it will not lower the self employment tax which is based on profits before retirement contributions.

There are two practical retirement plan options for the small business owner: the Simplified Employee Pension (SEP) and the KEOGH plans. Details on these plans and the advantages and disadvantages of each kind of plan is provided in Appendix g.

eg Because of its simplicity and minimal recordkeeping, the owner decided to establish a SEP. An owner can contribute up to 13% of net business income to the SEP which was done (.13 X 1005 = $131). See line 27 on 1040 form in Appendix g.

How Can You Deduct Health Insurance Premiums?

Currently self-employed persons are entitled to deduct 25% of their family health insurance premium provided they are not covered by another employer's plan. This deduction is taken as an adjustment to income on line 26 of the 1040 form and may not exceed the net income earned by the business (see Appendix f).

eg The owner is paying $3,000 per year

for family health insurance. Since neither the owner or spouse is covered under another employer's plan, they are entitled to a deduction of $750.

How Can Inventory Value Be Controlled?

Inventory value is controlled primarily by careful timing of purchases, stock reduction sales, and write-downs. It pays to keep inventory values as low as possible since (1) the cost of unsold goods is not deductible and increases taxable gain (2) unsold goods are regarded as assets which are taxable by many state or local jurisdictions (3) the cost of carrying inventory is very high and eats into profit margins.

The inventory valuation method best suited to the sideline businesses with modest inventories is known as the "lower of cost or market." That means the inventory is valued at whatever the cost to you was, unless for any reason it could not be sold at that price (damaged or obsolete) in which case the inventory is valued at whatever it could be sold for, including zero if it were totally worthless. Such inventory "write-downs" are done by entering the lower (market) value as the ending inventory on line 39 on the Schedule C. Naturally, any write-down must have back-up documentation and be reduced by insurance collected for the loss.

But which cost do you use when you've paid different amounts for the same item—a common occurence in businesses having large inventories. You simply make a selection between the LIFO and FIFO valuation. LIFO (Last In, First Out) *assumes* the goods sold were the last ones purchased. It doesn't matter if the actual goods sold were the ones purchased earlier at a lower price. Since prices rise over the long term, LIFO will usually result in a lower value for the remaining inventory and a lower taxable income. Incidently, changing evaluation methods requires IRS approval.

eg The owner's year-end purchase of merchandise was based on what could be sold quickly, recognizing that the cost of unsold goods is not deductible, and that carrying inventory is very high -- estimated to be 25% of the inventory value.

Are There Any Other Business Tax Benefits Available?

Businesses are allowed to deduct the cost of gifts (maximum $25 per individual per year) and contributions to community groups to promote good will. A business owner who is taking the standard deduction return rather than itemizing on the personal return, could make contributions in the name of the business.

The business can also deduct the cost of a safety deposit box and costs related to tax preparation which also benefit the sole proprietor as the financial accounts are so closely linked.

Certain tax credits are currently available for businesses hiring disadvantaged workers, building low income housing, rehabilitating older properties, using alternative energy sources, or conducting research. It's rare that such credits can be used by a small or sideline business, but such programs come and go and it's useful to review them each year just in case.

Credits are taken on line 44 of the 1040, and are often subject to AMT calculations.

A business owner having losses that exceed other income that year, can *carry back* any excess loss for as many as 3 years and obtain refunds of past taxes paid. If not used up in the carry back, the loss can be carried forward up to 15 years to reduce future taxes. Loss carry-backs are available only to tax payers who own businesses.

What Was The Owner's Total Financial Benefit?

The sideline business provided the owner the following financial benefits:

Use of Home (indirect cost)	$1849
Use of Personal Car (indirect cost)	572
Education (tuition, travel, books)	916
Meals for Owner (@ half meals cost)	337
Health Insurance Premium	750
Retirement Contribution	131
Salary to Family Member	480
Other (deposit box rent, tax help)	100
	$5135
Plus After-Tax Profit From Business ($1005 less 28% Federal, 7% State)	653
Total After-Tax Benefits	$5788

Note that to net as much from wages, the owner would have had to earn $10,092 because wages would have been subject to 7.65% Social Security and Medicare in addition to the 35% income taxes. The above powerfully illustrates the advantages of a sideline business even for persons of modest means.

Important! The information presented in this chapter is necessarily limited and subject to change. More complete and timely information is available free in IRS Publication #334, *Tax Guide to Small Businesses;* or at reasonable cost in commercially published tax guides that are usually more clearly written than Publication #334, and do a better job of highlighting and explaining tax saving opportunities. Your public library may subscribe to some good business periodicals that contain regular features on current and upcoming tax matters affecting small business.

Remember that even though you may use a tax preparer, you're the one responsible for keeping up with changes and opportunities that effect your bottom line. You can't plan and implement tax saving strategies that you learn about after the year has ended. Besides, unless you know what the preparer is suppose to be doing, you'll have little basis to judge the work being done on your behalf.

chapter 6

keeping your balance

What Are "Financials"?

When bankers or potential investors request the "financials," or financial statements, they are referring to the company's Profit & Loss (P&L) statement and Balance Sheet.

These two concise summaries reveal an enormous amount of information about the company's profitability, stability and financial strength. The information is vital to creditors as well as owners.

What Is A P&L Statement?

The P&L (Profit and Loss) statement is a summary of the financial performance of a business *over a period of time* (usually a month, quarter, or year). This report,

routinely requested by lenders, investors, and tax authorities, is the principal measure of performance. Sole proprietors need look no further than their Schedule C tax return for their Annual P&L figures, or their Financial Summaries for monthly and quarterly figures.

What Is A Reasonable Net Profit For A Business?

Over the long run the return should be at least equal to that of "no risk" investments such as insured Certificates of Deposits (CDs) or U.S. Treasury Notes. Therefore, it's not surprising that the national average for all businesses is 8% of total sales in recent

43

years. For example, a leading brewery recently reported 14% profit on sales; a leading oil company reported 5% and a leading grocery chain reported 2%. While these profit figures illustrate the common range of net profits, they are not comparable because they represent different industries. To be meaningful, profit comparisons must be made with similar businesses. For instance, net profits of small financial consultants, which are more similar to our business, are often in the 10-15% range.

eg The annual P&L statement for the company is shown below.

EconoGuides P&L Statement
(January 1 - December 31, 1991)

Gross Sales	*$10,860*
Less Returns	*63*
Net Sales	*10,797*
Cost of Goods Sold	*3,260*
Gross Profit	*7,537*
Consulting Services	*7,200*
Interest & Other	*180*
Total Income	*14,917*
Operating Expenses	*13,912*
Net Profit (before tax)	*$ 1,005*
Profit as % of Total Income	*6.7%*

FIGURE 17

Notice that a year's financial activity is neatly captured in less than a dozen lines. When used for internal management purposes, P&L statements usually show the profitability for each major product line. Costs that cannot be separated by product can be estimated using the percentage of total income each product represents. For

instance, Consulting Services is 48% of total income and assuming the percentage of total costs was the same, the profit from consulting was 7.2%; and the profit from book sales was 5.9%.

Why Do Profit Figures Get So Much Attention?

In addition to their obvious bottom line importance, profit margins can serve as indicators of business health much as temperature can indicate a person's health. Business failures are seldom the result of something sudden or unforeseen. Most often they are the result of a gradual erosion of profit margins that are ignored or accepted. A common scenario is a gradually increasing cost of production that is accompanied by increasing competition which prevents passing cost increases to the customer in product prices. The resulting squeeze on profits continues until there are no lenders willing to fund needed product or production improvements, or buyers willing to purchase what's left; and the business simply folds. One way to prevent this outcome is to monitor profit percentages closely and take corrective actions early.

eg The business's profit-loss statement indicates a pre-tax profit of 6.7% However this figure doesn't reflect the value of the owner's time which averaged 15 hours a week and totaled 750 hours. The $5,135 of reimbursements and benefits (see previous chapter) would only come to $6.85 per hour, which doesn't begin to reflect the value of the owner's services. This just means the business is being subsidized by the owner and has a long way to go before it can post a *true profit. Indeed, when the fair market value of the owner's service is applied, many sole proprietorships show no profit. This is an important consideration in valuing a sole proprietorship business (see discussion on Valuation later in this chapter).*

What Is A Balance Sheet?

The balance sheet is like a snapshot showing the business's financial condition on a *particular day* (usually the last day of a quarter or year).

A business is always in a balanced financial condition in one important respect: what it *owns* always equals what it *owes* to its creditors and its owners. Put another way, the creditors and owners have claims which are equal to the total value of the business. This balance, known as the accounting equation, can be expressed as follows:

Assets ➕ Liabilities ➖ Owner Equity

(what the business owns) (what it owes its creditors) (what it owes its owner)

The left side of the balance sheet usually shows the Assets, what the business has and what it's worth; and the right side shows to whom those assets belong. Note that if the Liabilities become greater than the Assets, the Owner Equity will be negative — which simply means the owner is responsible for paying off business creditors.

The balance sheet for the business is shown in Figure 18. Notice that the total Assets equal the total Liabilities plus Owner Equity ($6,290).

ECONOGUIDES BALANCE SHEET
(December 31, 1991)

ASSETS			LIABILITIES
CASH	$3,430	ACCOUNTS PAYABLE	$ 800
ACCOUNTS RECEIVABLES	600	NOTES PAYABLE	2,240
INVENTORY	340	TAXES PAYABLE	
PREPAID INS.	320	SALARIES PAYABLE	
TOTAL CURRENT	$4,690	TOTAL CURRENT	$3,040
FURNITURE & EQUIPMENT (LESS DEPRECIATION)		LONG TERM DEBT	$2,280
5,235		OWNER'S EQUITY	$ 970
(3,635)	$1,600		
TOTAL ASSETS	$6,290	TOTAL LIABILITIES	$6,290

FIGURE 18 The Balance Sheet

Where Do Balance Sheet Figures Come From?

■ CASH: This figure is the ending bank balance as of December 31 from the Annual Summary, ($3,430). If there are checks or cash on hand that hadn't yet been deposited, the total of such checks or cash would be included in this category.

■ ACCOUNTS RECEIVABLE: Total of sales invoices on the Accounts Receivable clipboard.

■ INVENTORY: From count or estimate; also shown on Annual Summary ($340).

■ PREPAID INSURANCE: From file containing insurance policies showing premiums and due dates. Since prepaid premiums can be converted to cash, they are included with other current assets. (File shows prepayments of $120 business and $200 auto insurance for total of $320).

■ CURRENT ASSETS: Current assets are those that can or will be converted to cash within one year.

■ OTHER ASSETS: Other assets include fixed or long term properties such as buildings and land, furniture and fixtures, office and transportation equipment, as well as intangible assets such as patents, copyrights, and trademarks.

■ FURNITURE AND EQUIPMENT: The figure shown is the cost of property less depreciation, which is also known as the "book value." The Annual Summary shows a cost of $5,235 and depreciation $3,635, making the current book value $1,600.

■ ACCOUNTS PAYABLE: Total of unpaid bills in the Expense folder at the end of December ($800).

■ NOTES PAYABLE: From Loan Record which shows loan payments due in the next 12 months are $800 for the computer and $1,440 on the truck for a total of $2,240. Note that the $500 bank loan was repaid.

■ TAXES PAYABLE: Federal, state, and local tax liabilities of the business. Income taxes on sole proprietorships are paid by owners on personal returns. The payroll taxes due on December's wages were paid December 31; so there are no taxes payable.

■ SALARY AND WAGES PAYABLE: Are amounts due for work done but not yet paid.

■ CURRENT LIABILITIES: Are business debts that must be paid within one year.

■ LONG TERM DEBT: Are business debts that are not due for at least a year. These normally include balances on mortgages, promissory and installment notes. The Loan Record indicates the balance remaining at the end of the next year will be $2,280.

■ OWNER EQUITY: Is the claim the owner has on the business assets, and is equal to the total Assets less current and long term liabilities ($6,290 - $5,320 = $970). This sum also reflects contributions made by the owner ($500).

What Can Be Learned From Balance Sheet Figures?

The figures on the balance sheet, and their relationship to each another (ratios), provides the owner and potential lender or investor such vital information as:

- the company's ability to pay its current debts or overcome a temporary financial crisis.

- the average number of days it takes to collect credit sales, reflecting the quality of receivables and effectiveness of collection procedures.

- how fast the company's product is moving, reflecting the success of the product and marketing efforts.

- the financial return that can be expected from investing in the company.

eg *An analysis of our Balance Sheet figures shows that:*

- *the business could operate for only one month without income.*

- *it takes an average of 30 days to collect on credit sales.*

- *the product appears to be successful and the inventory well managed.*

- *the overall financial condition is very weak, and investors or lenders would likely be unpersuaded (see Appendix i for explanation of how such information is obtained from balance sheet figures).*

How Can *Financials* Be Compared With Other Businesses?

Financial data can be directly compared with similar businesses by making P&L and balance sheet figures *common size*. This is done by converting figures to percentages: dividing all P&L figures by Net Sales; and all Balance Sheet figures by Total Assets. Comparing financial data can reveal conditions or trends which might otherwise go unnoticed. Comparable data are available from a variety of sources (see Appendix i).

Common size statements are also helpful in revealing the year-to-year changes within the business. Widely different annual sales and balance figures often conceal important trends that are quickly uncovered by common size percentages.

(Note): financial statements requested by banks and other creditors usually don't have to be audited by a Certified Public Accountant (CPA) if the proposed transaction is under $500,000.

eg *Selected P&L and Balance Sheet figures were converted to percentages (made common size) so they could be compared with the published percentages of similar businesses.*

Item	EconoGuides %	Comparable %
Cash	54	20
Accounts Receivable	10	25
Current Liabilities	48	20
Long-Term Liabilities	36	30
Cost of Goods Sold (P&L)	30	40

The above comparison suggests that our business has:

-higher percentage of cash
-lower percentage of receivables
-higher percentage of current debt
-lower production costs

If, say, we were seeking a loan or investors, we might consider using some cash to pay down current debt to bring the balance sheet more in line with the norms for similar businesses.

What Are Financial Projections?

Financial projections are forecasts and predictions business owners make to guide their day-to-day decisions. The process forces the owner to look and think ahead. By anticipating and planning for likely events the owner is prepared and has a measure of control as events unfold.

The financial projections routinely made are:

- budget
- cash flow
- inventory
- market value of business

How Is A Budget Constructed?

The budget is probably the best known and most widely used financial projection. A budget can be prepared by simply increasing each item on the previous year's Financial Summary (or Schedule C) by the expected inflation rate. However, this assumes operations will remain the same and new businesses are too dynamic for this approach. For them, a better method is to make some assumptions about changes that are needed or likely to occur, and adjust each income and expense item accordingly.

Budgeting requires more thinking than calculating. The difficult part is making realistic assumptions and sales forecasts and being realistic about the resources it will take to produce those results.

The usual tendency is to overestimate income and underestimate what it will cost to produce it. So, reality test your projections by asking yourself the "what if" questions a skeptical loan officer might ask. A realistic budget is the result of a lot of hard thinking and several trials and refinements. Don't expect to do it in one sitting. Happily, it does get easier as you accumulate more data and experience.

Budget construction begins by entering the figures from the Annual Summary in Column 1 of a worksheet (see Figure 19). Next, the percentage of total Income is computed for each item of income and expense by:

-dividing each figure by the total income,
-multiplying by 100, then
-rounding to the nearest whole number.

The resulting percentages are checked, rounded as needed to be sure they total 100%, and then entered in Column 2. The percentages can be used to estimate line item expenses when no better estimate is available. The basis of the forecast, whether these percentages or other, is noted in Column 3.

Next, Column 4 (Budget) is completed beginning with the income items. We expect to triple last year's product sales, and we'll be charging an additional 10% for the book ($11) in order to cover costs of inflation (we estimate will be about 6%) and the remainder for product upgrading, making the total estimated product income $35,800. The basis for our estimate (3 X + 10%) is noted in Column 3 in case we want to review or change it later.

We expect to double our consulting income, and adding 6% for inflation brings the total to $15,000 (rounded). Since our estimated income is approximately $50,000, our average monthly balance would be about $4,000 and could earn $200 interest during the year (4,000 X .05). Having completed the income estimates, we move to expenses.

To determine the estimated cost of materials, we find the total number to be sold by dividing the total product sales by the price of the product (35,800 ÷ 11 = 3,250). Next, we multiply the number to be sold by the estimated cost of each ($4) to get the total cost (3250 X 4 = 13,000). We note that the resulting cost of goods will be 36% of product sales. This percentage is higher than the previous year because we're upgrading the product but not passing on the extra cost. The 36% is considered acceptable because we know that the cost of goods in similar businesses is as much as 40% and probably reflects a better quality product.

From our experience and study of comparable businesses, we decide to increase advertising to 15% of total sales or $7,600.

Some expenses (Rent, Insurance, Interest and Depreciation) are known while others such as Repairs, Contract Services, Refunds, and Bank Charges, can be estimated from experience.

This year we will be employing our teenager 80 hours per month to process book orders, maintain inventories, and prepare bulk mailings, thereby freeing the owner to do the additional consulting work. We've budgeted for $480 per month ($6/hr) for salary. We know that payroll taxes will remain the same as last year which totaled 11.5% of salary.

For those expense categories that can be neither directly computed nor estimated, we multiply the percentage they represented of last year's income by the total budgeted income ($51,000). And since the budgeted income includes an allowance for inflation, the resulting figures need no further adjustment.

Finally, the last column (Quarterly Budget) is completed by dividing each budget item by 4. The quarterly budget column permits the owner to compare the "budgeted" amount with the "actual" quarter figures on the Financial Summary.

FINANCIAL SUMMARY				BUDGET '92	
Category	ACTUAL '91	%TOTAL INCOME	PROJECTION BASIS	ANNUAL	QUARTERLY
PRODUCTS	10,860	58	3X +10%	35,800	8,950
SERVICES	7,200	39	2X + 6%	15,000	3,750
INTEREST	139	1	4000@5%	200	50
MISCL	41				
SALES TAX					
INVENTORY	340	2			
NON-TAX					
INCOME	18,580	100		51,000	12,750
MERCHDSE	3,600	19	4X 3250	13,000	3,250
ADVERTISE	2,308	12	15% SALES	7,600	1,900
TELEPHONE	682	4	4%	2,000	500
OFFICE SUPP	924	5	5%	2,500	625
RENT	1,849	10	EST	1,900	475
MAINT/REP	48		EST	200	50
INSURANCE	120	1	EST	160	40
INTEREST	180	1	EST	240	60
CONTRACT	690	4	EST	1,500	375
CAR/TRUCK	1,344	7	7%	3,600	900
TRAVEL	568	3	3%	1,500	375
MEALS/ENT	540	3	3%	1,500	375
DUES/PUB	348	2	2X	700	175
REFUNDS	63		EST	200	50
SALES TAX					
BANK CHG	42		EST	60	15
MISCL	99	1	2X	200	50
WAGES	480	3	12 @480	5,800	1,450
PAYROLL	55		11.5% SAL	700	175
DEPRECIATE	3,635	20	EST	640	160
NON-DED					
EXPENSE	17,575	95		44,000	11,000
GAIN (LOSS)	1,005	5		7,000	1,750
TOTAL	18,580	100		51,000	12,750

FIGURE 19 Budget Worksheet

Any unexpected differences or trends can be spotted in ample time to take corrective actions and stay on top of events. Note that if the past year's earnings shown any seasonal variations, we would have computed the percentage of total sales earned in each quarter and applied those percentages to the total budget figures to determine the budgeted quarterly income.

Why Do You Need Cash Flow Projections?

Even with a good budget, it's possible to run out of cash; all it takes is for some receivables to lag and a few expenses to bunch up. An occasional short-fall is just an embarrassment, but a company that experiences frequent or unexpected cash shortages is not likely to survive. Such cash problems can be avoided by making a cash flow projection which uses budget figures to project *monthly cash balances*. The cash flow projection won't guarantee adequate cash, but it will identify which month(s) will be tight so the owner can adjust expenses or have time to look for and negotiate a temporary loan.

eg *The Cash Flow projection is constructed by setting up a worksheet as shown in Figure 20. Each budgeted income figure is divided by 12, rounded to the nearest $10, and entered for that category each month. For example, total product sale income is $35,800; dividing by 12 and rounding to nearest $10 yields $2,980 which is entered on the product sales line for each month. Next, income categories are totaled and the sum entered on the total income line for each month ($4,250).*

Next, the expenses that are payable in a particular month are entered. For example, rent and business insurance are payable in December (and will not show up on this projection) Auto insurance, expected to increase to $500 this year, and is payable in June ($250) and December ($250). However, the auto insurance cost is part of the $3,600 car/truck budget so the remaining ($3,100) is divided by 12 to get an estimated monthly operating expenses ($260).

We plan to make three merchandise (book) purchases of $3,250 each in January, May, and September. The payments will be made the month following the order. The remaining $3,250 merchandise expense is for the book mailers which will average $270 each month (see Appendix k, for Inventory calculations). We will make one bulk mailing (advertising) each quarter in January, April, July, and October. Bulk mailings must be paid for at the time of mailing. Payroll taxes will be paid in the month following each calendar quarter: April, July, October and December 31 (rather than January to simplify recordkeeping).

We expect other expenses will be constant and enter 1/12 of each item's annual budget for the estimated monthly expense. That done, expense categories are totaled and the sum entered on the Total Expense line. Next, the Gain or Loss is computed for each month by subtracting the Total Expense from the Total Income for that month.

Finally, the ending bank balance for each month is projected by adding the gain (or subtracting loss) from the beginning bank balance. Note that the beginning balance for January 1992 is the ending balance for

51

FINANCIAL SUMMARY			CASH FLOW '92		
Category	JAN	FEB	MAR	APR	MAY
Begin Balance	3,430	3,890	3,000	5,360	5,640
PRODUCTS	2,980	2,980	2,980	2,980	2,980
SERVICES	1,250	1,250	1,250	1,250	1,250
INTEREST	20	20	20	20	20
MISCL					
SALES TAX					
NON-TAX					
INCOME	4,250	4,250	4,250	4,250	4,250
MERCHDSE	270	3,520	270	270	270
ADVERTISE	1,900			1,900	
TELEPHONE	170	170	170	170	170
OFFICE SUPP	210	210	210	210	210
RENT					
MAINT/REP	20	20	20	20	20
INSURANCE					
INTEREST	20	20	20	20	20
CONTRACT	120	120	120	120	120
CAR/TRUCK	260	260	260	260	260
TRAVEL	120	120	120	120	120
MEALS/ENT	120	120	120	120	120
DUES/PUB	60	60	60	60	60
REFUNDS	20	20	20	20	20
SALES TAX					
BANK CHG					
MISCL	20	20	20	20	20
WAGES	480	480	480	480	480
PAYROLL				180	
EXPENSE	3,790	5,140	1,890	3,970	1,890
GAIN (LOSS)	460	⟨890⟩	2,360	280	2,360
End Balance	3,890	3,000	5,360	5,640	8,000

FIGURE 20 Cash Flow Projection

1991, and that each month's ending balance is entered as the beginning balance of the next month. Examining the projected cash flow, we conclude that after February we'll have comfortable bank balances, and by May we could safely transfer $2,000 to a money market mutual fund to get a higher yield.

Why Are Inventory Projections Important?

The cost of holding inventory has been estimated to be 25% of inventory value. What this means is that it would cost $1,000 just to *hold* $4,000 worth of inventory! Holding costs include: financing (15%), insurance (2%), property taxes (2%), handling (2%), obsolescence and shrinkage through loss or damage (4%).

So an important objective for the business owner is to hold just enough inventory to meet demand. Holding more reduces profits due to the holding costs; holding less reduces profits due to lost sales, back orders and customer dissatisfaction. Such inventory control is known as *Just In Time* inventory.

How Are *Just In Time* Inventory Levels Determined?

Surprisingly, quantity is not a reliable indicator of ideal inventory level because a large inventory can represent either additions needed to support *growing sales* or an accumulation due to *falling sales*. A better measure is *how* many times the inventory *turns over* in a given period. Turn-over is a more reliable indicator of

proper inventory level because when sales increase, turnover either increases or stays the same; when sales decrease, turnover decreases. So the business owner knows *when turnover decreases, the inventory level is too high.*

How Do You Know How Often Inventory Should Turn-Over?

In a start-up, it's usually a matter of trial and error, although some estimate can be made from data published for similar businesses. Aside from assuring optimum inventory level, the owner can reduce inventory costs by minimizing purchasing costs. This can be done by using formulas to determine the optimum order size, and reorder points (see Appendix k).

Most small businesses can track and control inventory during the year by visual inspection or indirectly by using the formula based on sales income. Physical counts are usually made at the end of the year for tax purposes. Retail businesses involving large or complex inventories usually rely on computerized, *continuous inventory* systems, which automatically calculate the new inventory balance each time a sale is made.

When Is A Market Valuation Of The Business Needed?

An estimate of the fair market value of the business is needed when:

- an owner wants to sell part or all of the business or take in a partner(s).

- business partners want to negotiate a buy-sell agreement in the event one partner decides to sell or dies.

- taxes are required on gifts or bequests involving ownership of the business.

The owner(s) can usually arrive at a value for the above purposes by using some *accepted rules of thumb* together with the Business Valuation form (Figure 21).

What Are Some Rules Of Thumb For Business Valuation?

For Minimum Value:

The Owner's equity
   OR

The sum needed to start a comparable business from scratch	(includes organization, promotion, equipment, supplies and capital)

For Maximum Value:

5 times *pretax* profit OR 7 times *after*tax profit OR	(Close to the historical price/earnings multiples of small company stocks)
0.1 to 1.0 times Gross Income + Inventory & Equipment	(The exact multiplier depends on the industry; 1.0 for very stable income such as CPA and insurance firms; 0.5 for restaurants and beauty salons; 0.3 for grocery stores; 0.1 for travel agencies)

How close proprietor businesses sell to the fair market valuation depends on whether the buyer feels the business is fully transferrable to a new owner. If not, the buyer would likely offer significantly less or request the owner stay on for a period of time as a paid manager or consultant. A former owner is often asked to sign an agreement to not compete for a stated time period.

Purchasers favor payments to owners for consulting and non-compete agreements as part of the purchase because such costs are deductible, whereas payments for the business's "goodwill" are not. See Appendix m for helpful hints on selling a business.

We want to project what the business might be worth by January 1995, when we expect to begin working in the business full time. We assume the 1992 budget will be met, that the business will double in 1993, and grow by 50% in 1994 (not unusual growth for a successful start-up). The projected figures are as follows:

P&L		
Total Income	=	*$ 150,000*
Total Expense	=	*$ 120,000*
Profit Margin	=	*$ 30,000*
Owner's Draw (pay)	=	*$ 20,000*
Net Profit Before Taxes	=	*$ 10,000*

BALANCE SHEET		
Working Capital	=	*$ 15,000*
Inventory	=	*$ 2,000*
Other Assets	=	*$ 10,000*
Owner's Equity	=	*$ 20,000*

Rules of thumb suggest the business should be worth between $20,000 (owner's equity) and $50,000 (5 X pretax profit). Using the valuation form shown in Figure 21, the calculated value is $36,000. This works out to about 0.2 X Gross Income + Inventory & Equipment, and appears reasonable given the nature of the business.

BUSINESS VALUATION
(1-1-95)

1 INCOME

   A. Total Income (less returns)   *150,000*

   B. Total Expense (cost of goods sold plus operating less interest & depreciation)   *120,000*

   C. Owner Salary (for a Sole Proprietorship, what a manager would be paid)   *20,000*

   D. Income (A - B + C)   *10,000*

2 ASSETS & CAPITAL

   A. Building & Land

   B. Furnishings

   C. Equipment   *10,000*

   D. Inventory (raw & finished)   *2,000*

   E. Other

   F. Total Assets   *12,000*

   G. Working Capital (current assets less current liabilities)   *15,000*

   H. Assets & Capital (F + G)   *27,000*

3 EARNINGS

   A. Income (1D)   *10,000*

   B. Alternate Return (2H X current interest: inflation plus 4%)   *2,000*

   C. Earnings (A - B)   *8,000*

4 MULTIPLE

   A. Income (0 = unsure 5 = assured)   *2*

   B. Competition (0 = high 5 = none)   *3*

   C. Company (0 = start-up 5 = known)   *3*

   D. Industry (0 = decline 5 = growth)   *4*

   E. Multiple (A + B + C + D/4)   *3*

5 VALUE

   A. Assets (2F)   *12,000*

   B. Earnings Multiple (3C X 4E)   *24,000*

   C. Market Value (A + B)   *36,000*

FIGURE 21 Finding The Value Of The Business

How Does The Financial System Keep Up With Business Growth?

The financial system described is capable of efficiently processing large numbers of transactions and dollars. However, you can expect every aspect of the system will grow along with the rest of the business; that means increasingly more checks, more invoices, more records and, happily, more money to manage and invest. To keep ahead of it all, you'll want to consider adding one or more of the following options as needs arise:

- One-Write system
- bookkeeping services
- automated program
- petty cash fund
- purchase order system
- investment account(s)

See Appendix 1 for additional information on implementing the above options.

chapter 7

getting personal

How Much Are You Saving?

An annual summary of personal income and expenses is the P&L statement for personal finances; the bottom line is *savings*. Spending and savings figures can be compared with the experience of others just as with the business statement. And, like the business, the personal statement serves as the basis for tax returns, budgets and planning. Personal financial summaries are normally made only once a year. The ideal time is at the beginning of the year soon after all wage, interest and other statements for the previous year have been received; but a good working estimate can be made any time using the information from the most recent three month period.

How Do You Make A Personal Financial Summary?

The procedure is the same as that used in preparing the business financial summary:

1. Establish Income and Expense Categories

Household accounts are all pretty much the same and the categories shown in Figure 22, and detailed in Appendix c, can probably be used with minor modifications as needed.

2. Find Totals For Each Income Category

Enter income from W-2, 1099, interest and dividend statements, Schedule C, and other forms or records in the appropriate income category and total.

e̶g̶ Note how the $1,005 net profit from the business is included as income, while reimbursement for business use of home and personal auto ($2,421) is included in the non-taxable income category.

3. Find Totals For Each Expense Category

Sort year's canceled checks, credit card slips, and cash receipts by expense categories. Enter totals in the appropriate expense category.

e̶g̶ Taxes withheld ($9,300) include federal ($3,830), state ($2,142), and Social Security and Medicare taxes ($3,328). Note that sales tax is accounted for in other categories by using total purchase prices which include sales taxes.

The housing expense ($8,900) includes mortgage payments ($7,200), maintenance ($500), real estate taxes ($800) and insurance ($400). Utilities include heat, lights, water and sewer ($1,600) plus telephone ($605) expenses.

Transportation expenses contain the costs of *owning and operating the owner's personal car, including the cost related to business use which was reimbursed.*

The savings figure includes IRA and SEP contributions ($2,130), the equity the owner accrued in the business during the year ($970 which includes the owner's $500 contribution), and $1,400 in savings which includes interest earned.

4. Find Percent of Total Income For Each Category

Divide each income and expense category by total income ($47,440) to find the percentage each category represents of total income. Enter percentage in column 4, rounding to the nearest whole number; check to be sure total equals 100%.

5. Compare Percentages with Published Averages

Enter comparable percentage figures from published averages (by the Tax Foundation, Census Bureau, popular financial magazines and newspapers) in column 5.

Categories that are significantly higher or lower than published averages should be checked carefully to be sure you're not overlooking some important aspect of that expenditure. The object is not to match your spending to everyone else, but to find out why yours is so different for this category.

e̶g̶ We find reasonably good agreement with national average figures with the exception of taxes, housing, insurance and savings. The lower taxes are the result of

Category	OWNER	SPOUSE	TOTAL	%	COMPARABLE %
Begin Balance					
WAGES	30,000	13,500	43,500	92	
INTEREST	257	257	514	1	
BUSINESS	503	502	1,005	2	
NON-TAX	1,211	1,210	2,421	5	
INCOME	31,971	15,469	47,440	100	
TAXES			9,300	20	30
HOUSING			8,900	19	13
UTILITIES			2,205	5	4
PERS. INSUR.			2,150	5	2
FOOD			4,930	10	11
CLOTHING			2,945	6	5
HEALTHCARE			4,290	9	9
TRANSPORT			2,615	6	7
RECREATION			2,510	5	5
EDUCATION			1,135	2	2
CONTRIBUTE			800	2	2
OTHER			1,160	2	5
SAVINGS			4,500	9	5
EXPENSE			47,440	100	100

PERSONAL FINANCIAL SUMMARY '91

FIGURE 22 Personal Financial Summary

self-employment deductions, IRA contributions, and non-taxable reimbursements which reduced taxable income; also helping were below average state income tax rates.

The higher housing cost is explained by the owner's 20 year fixed-rate mortgage whose annual cost is higher than the more popular 30 year adjustable, and even more so in periods of falling interest rates. The higher insurance costs is likely due to the owner's comprehensive life and disability coverage; it is generally conceded that most families are under-insured for such risks.

The owner's savings rate of 9% is nearly twice the national average of 5%. However, the national average ranges from 0%, for many persons under 25 years of age to over 15% for many over 65 years of age. In addition, the U.S. savings rate is acknowledged to be low compared with other leading industrialized nations where savings average about 10%. When viewed from these perspectives, the 9% rate is just average, and could be improved.

If the savings rate had been unusually or unacceptably low, we would try to reduce expenses, examining first those categories having above average spending and those which represent more than 5% of total income. If the savings rate had been unusually high, we would want to be sure we weren't neglecting some important area, be it insurance or recreation. When examining a category having lower than average spending, consider first if the lower cost could be due to cash purchases for which no records were kept.

Important! Household expenditures should be made by check or credit card whenever possible, assuming you have free checking and pay off credit card balances each month. These records will enable you to track expenditures and pinpoint areas for potential savings. Some deluxe credit cards and financial management accounts at banks and brokerages provide an annual summary by expense category as part of the service which saves you the time and trouble.

If you plan to itemize deductions on your tax return, separate and save the appropriate canceled checks and receipts; you'll want proof of tax payments, mortgage and other tax deductible interest payments, medical and job related expenses, tax deductible donations, IRA and other plan contributions. Be sure to keep copies of any W-2, 1099 and other income forms sent you as well as a copy of your completed 1040 Return with all the Schedules.

You don't have to wait until the end of the year to get a handle on personal finances. Just sort your canceled checks, credit card slips and other receipts for the past 3 months. Estimate your weekly cash outlay for food, transportation, and miscellaneous expenses. Multiply these weekly cash estimates by 12 (3 months) and add these totals to the proper expense category. Now, multiply each category total by 4 to get the estimated annual expense. Total all expense categories and subtract from your expected annual income to find your estimated savings. Then, compare spending and savings figures with published averages as described.

How Much Are You Worth?

Like the business balance sheet, a net worth statement is a snapshot of personal assets and liabilities as of a given day. Net worth statements are routinely required by mortgage companies, banks and other lenders as part of personal and business loan applications. They also serve as mileposts of financial progress, and are virtually indispensable in the end game of estate planning.

Just as lenders use balance sheet ratios to judge whether a company is credit worthy, similar measures are applied to net worth statements. For example: cash assets should be at least 2 times the total of current liabilities; mortgage payments should not exceed 25%-28% of take home pay, or a home costing no more than 1.5 to 2 times annual earnings; short term or installment loans should total less than 15% of take home pay; and the combined short term and mortgage payments should not exceed 35% of take home pay; personal property, a depreciating asset, should be less than 15% of total assets.

Net worth statement figures can be gotten quickly and easily by using the following guidelines:

■ CASH - Latest account balances.

■ SECURITIES - Latest balance on mutual fund statements; closing stock, bond, and precious metal prices quoted in newspaper; face value of bonds you intend to hold to maturity or bid price reported in newspaper; the amount you paid for limited partnerships.

■ INSURANCE - Cash value according to the table in the policy.

■ PERSONAL PROPERTY

Home—insured value plus lot value; recent sales price of comparable house in area; or number of square feet multiplied by current cost per square foot plus cost of land.

Cars and Recreation Vehicles—loan value less 15% (from any bank or insurer).

Boat—purchase price less 30% first year and 10% each year thereafter.

Aircraft—loan value (from any insurer).

Collectibles—50% of purchase price, 70% if held over 5 years.

Jewelry—30% of purchase price.

Other personal assets—usually 15% and not more than 25% of purchase price.

■ RETIREMENT PLANS - Latest balance on IRA, SEP, and KEOGH accounts; vested interest in company 401(k) or pension plan (supplied by employer).

Furnishing a net worth statement means revealing private and perhaps sensitive personal financial information. For this reason, many persons submit partial statements listing just enough of their assets to show they are credit worthy. Naturally, all liabilities must be reflected, but are usually grouped under broad headings to keep from revealing more detail than is necessary.

The owner's Net Worth statement is shown in Figure 23. Note how the owner's equity in the business is reported as a

61

NET WORTH
(December 31, 1991)

ASSETS		LIABILITIES	
CASH		**CURRENT**	
Checking	$1,600	Bills Due	$ 300
Money Market	5,000	Credit Card	700
CD	2,000	Installment Note	1,000
Subtotal Cash	8,600	Subtotal Current	2,000
SECURITIES		**LONG TERM NOTES**	
U.S. Bonds	3,000		
EconoGuides	1,000		
PERSONAL PROPERTY			
1988 Automobile	5,000	Automobile	0
Furnishings	5,000		
Jewelry	2,000		
Other	2,000		
REAL ESTATE			
Residence	70,000	Home Mortgage	59,000
RETIREMENT FUNDS			
IRA	8,600		
SEP	100		
Employer 401 (k)	6,700		
TOTAL ASSETS	$112,000	**TOTAL LIABILITY**	$ 61,000
NET WORTH (ASSETS - LIABILITIES)			51,000

FIGURE 23 Owner's Net Worth Statement

personal asset. As owner's equity represents net value, it's not necessary to list the individual business assets and liabilities on the personal statement. Note also that the owner's balance in the business's SEP retirement plan is listed as a personal asset.

With $8,600 in cash assets and only $2,000 in current liabilities, the owner could qualify for an additional $2,000 short term loan because cash assets would be 2 times current liabilities.

The home equity of $11,000 ($70,000 - 59,000), would qualify the owner for an $8,000 home equity loan (the maximum typically being 70% to 80% of the equity). Such loans are attractive because interest payments are tax deductible, but processing costs can be high and an owner risks losing the home if some unforseen difficulty prevents timely payments.

Another strength of owner's statement is that depreciating personal property ($14,000) is about 12% of total assets, which means the remaining 88% asset value can be expected to either remain stable or appreciate.

Are You Saving Enough?

The tables shown in Figure 24 can be used to determine how much you must save each year in order to achieve your financial goals, be they a down-payment on a home, college education, or a new car. Here's how:

1. Determine the goal, in present dollars, and the time available to save.

The owners want to give their daughter her choice of a good used car when she graduates college in 5 years; such a car can currently be purchased for $5,000.

2. Find the probable future cost by estimating the annual inflation rate during the savings period and applying the appropriate figure in the Inflation Multiples Table (Figure 24A) to the present purchase price.

The owners expect the inflation rate to average 4% per year over the next 5 years; the inflation multiple, from the Table, is 1.22, meaning the cost of a comparable car 5 years from now would be $6,100 (5,000 X 1.22).

3. Find the amount that has to be saved each year by estimating the *annual after tax* return on savings, and applying the appropriate figure in the Compound Interest Table (Figure 24B) to the future cost. The after tax return is used because the purchase must be made with dollars remaining after paying tax on income earned by the investment.

The owners estimate they can earn 6% after tax on their investment since they can put the funds in longer term investments. The Compound Interest table indicates every dollar added each year will total of 5.98 at the end of 5 years. By dividing the 5.98 into the total dollars needed ($6,100), the owners find they will need to invest $1,020 each year (6,100 ÷ 5.98).

63

Yrs	3%	4%	5%	6%	7%	8%	10%
5	1.16	1.22	1.28	1.34	1.40	1.47	1.61
10	1.34	1.48	1.63	1.79	1.97	2.16	2.59
15	1.56	1.80	2.08	2.40	2.76	3.17	4.18
20	1.81	2.19	2.65	3.21	3.87	4.66	6.73
25	2.09	2.67	3.39	4.29	5.43	6.85	10.83
30	2.43	3.24	4.32	5.74	7.61	10.06	17.45

Figure 24A Inflation Multiples At Various Annual Rates

Yrs	3%	4%	5%	6%	7%	8%	10%
5	5.47	5.64	5.80	5.98	6.16	6.34	6.72
10	11.81	12.51	13.21	13.97	14.81	15.65	17.53
15	19.16	20.91	22.66	24.67	27.00	29.32	34.95
20	27.68	31.20	34.72	38.99	44.21	49.42	63.00
25	37.55	43.83	50.11	58.16	68.56	78.95	108.18
30	49.00	59.38	69.76	83.80	103.07	122.35	180.94

Figure 24B One Dollar Per Year Compounded Annually

Will You Be Able To Retire?

The Personal Financial Summary and Net Worth statements tell us where we are and how we're doing. What most people also want to know is, given their present course, will they have enough to retire. Here's the procedure:

1. How much will you need to live on when you retire? The rule of thumb is that persons need between 70%-80% of their pre-retirement earnings to maintain their living standard in retirement.

The owner's current earnings are about $45,000 and at 70% would require a retirement income of about $32,000 per year (note figures used in retirement calculations are before tax).

2. How much social security or employer pension payments can you expect? Your savings are typically one leg of the three-legged stool supporting most retirees, with social security and employer plans being the other two legs.

The owners send post card form (SSA 7004) to the Social Security Administration who quickly estimate their retirement benefits will total about $12,000 per year (close to the average benefit). This will reduce the amount needed from their own savings to $20,000 per year (32,000 - 12,000).

3. How much retirement income can be expected from present savings and assets? Assume your current assets and savings will keep pace with inflation and can then be depleted over your retirement.

Assuming the owners' present $50,000 retirement savings and assets (net worth) kept pace with inflation, it could provide $2000 per year for 25 years (to age 90) which reduces the annual amount needed to $18,000 (20,000 - 2,000).

4. How much must be saved each year to reach retirement goal? Make a realistic estimate of the average, before tax, return your investments can earn, and divide this figure into annual sum needed to find the amount of savings needed.

The owners estimate they could earn an average of 8% before taxes and find they would need to save a total of $225,000 to yield the $18,000 per year needed at retirement (18,000 ÷ .08).

Next, determine the number of years until retirement and estimate what the annual inflation rate might average during this period. Use the Inflation Table to find the amount of future dollars needed to equal today's purchasing power.

The owners plan to retire in 20 years. Although inflation has averaged around 6% per year during the last 20 years, some authorities are predicting lower inflation rates in the future, so the owners decide to use 4% as an average inflation rate. Looking at the Inflation Multiples table under 20 years and 4%, they find the figure 2.19 which represents the number of future dollars needed to equal the purchasing power *of today's dollar. This means that in 20 years it will take $492,750 to buy what $225,000 would buy today (225,000 X 2.19).*

Now, use the Compound Interest table to find how much must be saved *each year* in order to reach the sum needed.

🔖 *At 20 years and 8% is the figure 49.42 (the value of one dollar compounded at that rate for that period of time). Dividing this figure into the required future sum ($492,750) yields the amount the owners must save each year ($9,970).*

5. Compare current savings to retirement needs and make necessary adjustments to budget or retirement plans. If current savings cannot be increased sufficiently to meet projections, retirement plans can be altered. For instance, retirement can be postponed to allow more time to build savings; retirees can plan to work part-time to supplement their other retirement income; or living costs might be reduced by moving and economizing.

Saving for long term goals (like college education and retirement) requires great discipline because the goals and sums involved seem beyond reach. It is an understandable, but serious and irreversible mistake, to postpone saving for long term needs. The fact is that time is the indispensable ingredient which compounds modest savings into the sizeable sums required to meet long term goals. In this sense, time is money and savings for both short and long term goals must be done simultaneously.

🔖 *In addition to the current annual savings of $4,500, the owner is saving a total of $3,000 in an employer matched contribution 401(k) plan. The total savings of $7,500 is still $2,470 short of the amount needed (9,970 - 7,500). The owners decide the shortfall is too great to be made up in cutting expenses, and decide the spouse will look for additional work.*

Are You Maximizing The Return On Your Savings?

Historical data shows the lowest returns were from "cash" investments such as CD's Treasury Bills and Money Market Funds. Only slightly better were corporate and government "bonds". The highest returns by far were from "stocks" which, unlike the fixed return cash and bond investments, were able to keep well ahead of inflation. Professional investment managers aim for a return that will average 2% more than the long term inflation rate. History and experience show it is not possible to get such results without a significant percentage of stocks in the investment mix. And while it's true that higher returns carry higher risks, the risk can be minimized. Besides, a small current risk is better than a guaranteed loss over time.

🔖 *The owner's Net Worth Statement indicates savings investments, including retirement funds, of $26,400, of which 60% are cash, 25% bonds and 15% stocks. The 85% in fixed return investments, while providing short term safety and peace of mind, exposes the owner's savings to the long* *term ravages of inflation. A more appropriate allocation, based on age, income and conservative investment philosophy of the owner would be: 45% stocks, 45% bonds and 10% cash. The owner can use "dollar cost averaging" to gradually convert cash to stock and bond investments and ensure that purchases will be at a reasonable price (see Appendix r).*

How Can You Minimize Investment Risks?

Investment risk has been estimated to be 70% company related and 30% market related. Company risk is minimized by spreading the investment among many companies, an approach known as *diversification*. Market risk is minimized by *allocation* of funds among stocks, bonds and cash so the investment is protected whichever way the market moves. Both company and market risk can be minimized by allocating the investment among stock, bond and money market *mutual funds* as these funds are composed of many different companies and assets. The risk can be further reduced by investing in funds that are comprised mainly of blue chip stocks, top rated corporate bonds and U.S. Treasury issues.

Another proven strategy for minimizing risk is "buy and hold." Historically, the risk of loss has been close to zero when stocks were held more than ten years. The strategy was recently reaffirmed in a study showing that virtually all stock gains were achieved during a few, brief periods of high appreciation. To avoid being out of the market during these infrequent surges, the long term investor must learn to ignore the inevitable short term fluctuations (see Appendix r).

Do You Have A Financial Plan?

The following prioritized checklist is intended to stimulate your thinking and guide your personal financial planning:

1. Obtain major medical insurance coverage.

2. Obtain term life insurance if you have dependents (use 5 to 7 times annual take home pay as a rough guide if family has no other source of income or assistance).

3. Purchase car and household furnishings (don't exceed 15% of net worth, consider the used market).

4. Purchase auto and renters insurance (high deductibles and no frills will help keep premiums down).

5. Build a reserve cash fund of 3 month's earnings (6 months for persons with higher incomes).

6. Upgrade medical coverage to comprehensive plan (use high deductible to lower premiums).

7. If not covered by employer, purchase disability insurance (equal to minimum monthly living expenses; choose 6 month waiting period to lower premium).

8. Start savings program, use employer 401(k) or 403(b) plans if available.

9. Purchase starter home (stay within 1.5 times annual income using minimum down payment).

10. Upgrade car and furnishings (stay within 15% of net worth).

11. Start savings fund for children using tax advantaged accounts, variable annuities, Series E savings bonds or zero coupon bonds.

12. Start investment portfolio using IRA, KEOGH, variable annuities and other tax deferred vehicles. Begin with fixed-return investments like money market mutual funds, ginnie mae and zero coupon bonds.

13. Upgrade home or purchase second home (keep mortgage payments under 25% of take home pay); shorten 30 year mortgages to 20 years through monthly pre-payments.

14. Expand and diversify investment portfolio (add stock and bond mutual funds according to suggested allocation percentages).

15. Add to taxed-advantaged accounts for children over 14 with tax-free gifts or Series E Bonds which are tax free when used for tuition payments.

16. Adjust insurance protection as needed. Build up of assets usually permits reduction of life and disability protection but requires additional liability protection.

17. Transition investment portfolio to retirement allocations emphasizing high quality stocks and bonds, and annuities.

18. Begin estate planning using gifts and simple trusts to maximize tax benefits and reduce impact of probate (see Appendix s for details).

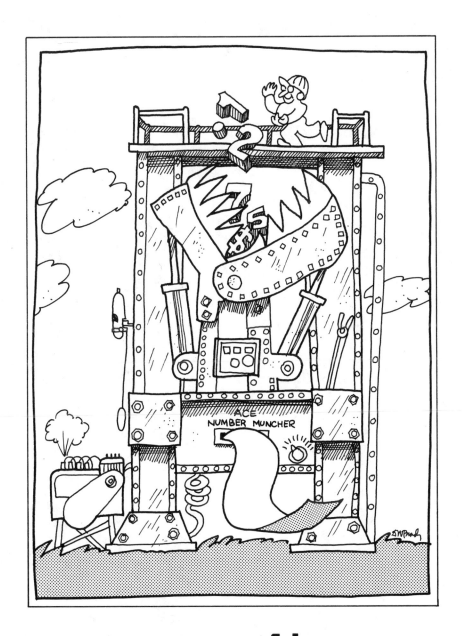

appendix

Legal Forms Of Business

Sole Proprietorship

What?
One owner business.

Why?
Advantages: The sole proprietorship is the simplest form of business, with minimal paperwork, and maximum independence. The owner makes all decisions and reaps all rewards.

Disadvantages: The owner is fully responsible for all mistakes. There is no distinction between business assets and personal assets such as the owner's residence, automobile, savings and retirement accounts. Everything the owner owns is at risk if the business should fail.

How?
There are usually no requirements to setting up a business which will operate under your own name. If it is to operate under a business name, some states or counties require filing a "fictitious name" or "DBA" (doing business as) form with the state or county clerk's office. Financial statements required by lenders usually must show personal as well as business assets and liabilities. Sole proprietorships automatically terminate when the owner leaves or dies.

Tax Filing?
The sole proprietor pays Federal income taxes by filing Schedules C and SE with the 1040 form (and appropriate state income tax forms where applicable). For detailed information on recordkeeping and filing tax returns for sole proprietorships, write for IRS publication #334.

Recordkeeping?
No modifications required.

Partnership

What?
A partnership is two or more persons who join together to carry on a trade or business. Partners may be identified or unidentified (silent); and either actively or not actively involved in running the business.

Why?
Advantages: Partnerships bring additional funds, energy, and complementary knowledge and skills to the enterprise. For instance, one partner may contribute the technical or creative

ideas while the other may contribute the financial resources and know-how to bring the product to life and market it successfully.

Disadvantages: like the sole proprietorship, a partner's personal assets are not distinguishable from the business assets and are fully at risk in a partnership. Also, a partner is *personally responsible for the acts of other partners*. Therefore, one partner can bankrupt the business and all the partners as well. Other disadvantages include more paperwork and less independence, because decisions must be shared with other partners.

How?

A partnership comes into being by executing a partnership agreement. While not a legal requirement, nearly all partnerships are based on a written agreement. Because of the unlimited personal liability each partner assumes, this document should be prepared by an attorney experienced in drafting partnership agreements. Such agreements normally include:

- how much each partner will contribute and share in profits or losses (it's not unusual for partners to share profits in proportion to amount of funds or time contributed, but to share losses equally).

- how much money each partner will be able to draw from the business (known as Guaranteed Payment).

- provisions in event of voluntary withdrawal or death. Like sole proprietorships, partnerships are automatically terminated upon death of one of the partners. That's why agreements usually include "buy and sell" clauses outlining how partners may be bought out. Life insurance policies naming other partner(s) as the beneficiary are often used to provide funds for buyouts in order to keep the business going until a new partnership is formed.

Tax Filing?

While the partnership itself does not pay taxes, it is required to <u>file</u> an annual tax return (Form 1065) with a Schedule (K-1) showing each partner's taxable income (loss) and the amount subject to Self Employment Tax (SE). Each partner reports the income and taxes due on the appropriate schedule of the personal return (1040). The partnership form (1065) and Schedules can be complicated requiring a professional tax preparer.

Recordkeeping?

Capital contributed by each partner; otherwise no other modifications required. Additional information on tax filing and recordkeeping for Partnerships, in the IRS publication #541.

Important! The Partnership described is also known as a *general partnership*. In recent years a hybrid form known as the *limited partnership* has become common, especially in connection with tax-advantaged investments. The limited partnership allows partners to invest without assuming the unlimited liability of the general, or operating, partners. Instead, the limited partner's liability is limited to the amount invested in the business. Limited partnerships are subject to substantial organizational costs and governmental reporting requirements, and not usually an option for the small start-up business.

Corporation

What?
A corporation is a legal entity separate from its owners and, like a living being, responsible for its own life. The corporation may be closed (closely held) meaning it's owned by a small group, or it may be open, meaning that stock in the company is sold openly—allowing large numbers of people to become part owners.

Advantages: The principal benefit, and some argue the <u>only</u> reason to incorporate, is limited liability; that is, the owners' personal assets are not at risk. The owner's relationship to the corporation can be likened to parents of an adult child—they gave it life, but are not responsible for its mistakes or obligations. Other advantages include the ability to:

▪ easily increase or change the ownership including passing it on to heirs.

▪ hire owners as employees thereby providing deductible but non-taxable benefits such as accident, health and life insurance among others;

▪ accumulate earnings rather than having to distribute 100% of profits;

▪ enter lease agreements with owners for rent of facilities and equipment belonging to the owner or lower-taxed family members;

▪ earn non-taxable income on investments in common stock or stock funds (currently 70% of stock dividends are non-taxable to corporations).

Disadvantages: A major disadvantage of incorporation is double taxation of corporate earnings. The corporation pays income taxes on its earnings, then the stockholder and owners pay personal income taxes on those same earnings (dividends). There is considerable additional paperwork including corporate minutes and resolutions documenting decisions, as well as State and Federal Corporate Tax Returns. Owners are not protected from negligent acts of the corporate officers or employees and are frequently asked to co-sign corporate notes making them personally liable for repayment of the loan (which nullifies the limited liability protection of the corporate form). Personal Service Corporations (where income is from professional services: such as doctors, lawyers, accountants, actuaries, engineers, consultants, and performers) are currently taxed at a higher rate than the personal tax rate.

How?
Incorporation papers are filed with the state. Average cost, with attorney assistance, is about $500; without attorney assistance about $200, including seal and stock certificates. Annual incorporation fees usually depend on earnings and can be several hundred dollars.

Tax Filing?
A corporation must file and pay corporate income taxes (Federal Form 1120). Dividend payments are documented on Form 1099 DIV which is sent to payees who include the amount on their personal returns (Federal Form 1040). Corporations are also subject to, and must file state and, where applicable, local income taxes.

Recordkeeping?
Changes include: "Owner Contributions" to "Stock Sales"; "Owners Draw" to "Officer Salary". Add: "Benefits" expense. For additional information on recordkeeping and filing taxes for corporations, write the IRS for publication #542.

Important! Because of double taxation, most corporate owners pay themselves maximum deductible wages in order to minimize taxable corporate earnings. However, such wages and benefits must be comparable to what others in similar fields and similar experience are earning. Otherwise, the IRS can charge that the excessive wages and benefits are really disguised dividends, which are subject to double taxation. The corporate form makes good sense for businesses where liability protection is important, such as construction and manufacturing, and where annual earnings will be taxed at <u>less</u> than personal rates and can be accumulated.

In closely held corporations, real estate and equipment is best kept in the owner's name and rented to the corporation under a net lease agreement where the corporation pays for maintenance, repair, and insurance in addition to a reasonable rental fee. Such rental income can be largely offset by depreciation and interest expenses minimizing the owner's tax liability. Alternatively, some owners place rental assets in the names of lower-taxed family members such as children over 14 (or under 14 if earnings amount to less than $1,000 per year) or retired family members on limited incomes.

S-Corporation

What?
The S-Corporation is a hybrid between a regular corporation, also known as a C- Corporation, and a partnership.

Advantages: The S-Corporation combines the desirable limited liability of a corporation with the desirable single taxation of the partnership. Losses, common during start-up years, are deductible on the shareholders' personal returns, reducing their personal taxes. Furthermore, if losses exceed $3,000, they can be *carried back* to prior years on personal returns even if the S-Corporation is only one year old. S-Corporations provide an easy way to transfer income to lower taxed family members; the owner simply gives such members stock in the corporation.

Disadvantages: Owners of S-Corporations are not employees and not entitled to tax-advantaged employee benefits. In addition, some states don't recognize S-Corporations and tax them as regular corporations.

How?

In order to qualify for S-Corporation status, there can be no more than 35 shareholders and there can be no corporate shareholders. A regular corporation can switch to a S-Corporation and *visa versa* by following IRS guidelines.

Tax Filing?

The S-Corporation is required to file a return (Form 1120S) but is not required to pay taxes. Instead, it completes a Schedule K-1 reporting the profit or loss for each shareholder. The shareholders in turn report these figures on their personal 1040 forms.

Recordkeeping?

Recordkeeping is similar to that of partnerships and no other modifications are necessary for the S-Corporation. For additional information on S-Corporations, see IRS publication #589 and consult your state tax office.

Important! The most appropriate legal form for your business depends a lot on how much money your business is earning and how exposed you are to lawsuits. The tax reform acts of recent years, have reduced the tax advantages of one legal form over another. Still, if a change in legal form is advisable, the timing can result in considerable tax savings. Say, for example you've been thinking about incorporating your small retail or manufacturing business and you're forecasting a very profitable year. It would pay to incorporate as soon in the tax year as possible to take advantage of the corporation's ability to retain earnings at the favorable tax rates (15% for first $50,000 as opposed to 33% personal rates). On the other hand, your business may be a Corporation expecting losses in excess of present or past earnings. In this case, it may be wise to change to a S-Corporation as soon as possible so those losses can be used to offset personal income.

To Sum Up:

■ Pension and profit share advantages are similar for all legal forms.

■ Partnerships and S-Corporations must file returns, but pass on gains or losses directly to owners. These forms of business are useful in start up and early stages when losses are common. The S-Corporation provides a simple means of raising capital, shielding personal assets from liability, and transferring business assets to family members.

■ Manufacturing and retailing corporations can accumulate earnings at favorable tax rates to a maximum of $250,000. Personal assets are shielded and owners get tax advantaged benefits. The disadvantages are double taxation of dividends, additional expenses for paperwork, bookkeeping, tax preparation, and annual fees.

■ While Personal Service Corporations are permitted to accumulate $150,000 in earnings, they are currently subject to an initial 34% tax rate which is higher than current personal tax rates.

■ Review the legal form of your business in light of any announced changes in your business or government regulations.

Keeping Track Of Accounts Receivable

After the product or service is delivered, the original invoice is sent to the customer, and a duplicate copy is put on an Accounts Receivable clipboard (Figure 25). Invoices are kept on the clipboard in numerical order, which is also date ordered. When payment is received, the duplicate is marked paid, dated, and placed in the 9" x 12" manila envelope containing records for the current month.

If payment is not received by the due date, the customer is contacted. The kind of contact (card, letter, phone call) and date is noted on the <u>back</u> of the invoice. If the customer says they've not received the invoice, a photocopy is sent. *Your invoice copy should never leave the clipboard until it has been paid.* Overdue invoices will be on the top, making it easy to see which require follow-up action. Record date and response to collection attempts and the name and number of contact person on the back of the invoice.

The amount owed your business at any given time is simply the total of all the invoices on the clipboard. Since the Accounts Receivable clipboard represents "money *nearly* in the bank", care is needed to prevent misplacing it or any of the invoices.

If you expect to have only occasional credit sales, you can have the Invoice form in the appendix photocopied (fold form and insert carbon paper to make a duplicate copy for clipboard). If you expect numerous credit sales you'll save billing time by using pre-numbered, two-part invoice forms with imprinted return address, and double window envelopes.

Adding interest charges to overdue invoices has a way of speeding up payments. Some businesses price their products and services so they can offer a small discount (1% or so) for payments received within 10 days. In any event, you can expect to have a few delinquent accounts, and it's better to price your product so you can easily absorb this small loss rather than getting upset or wasting time trying to collect. Common payment terms are NET 10 or NET 20 which means bills are due 10 or 20 days from date of billing. Your payment terms should be noted on your invoice.

The following collection procedure usually works well: when a bill is 2 weeks overdue, send a pre-printed reminder post card; after 4 weeks, a phone call or letter requesting immediate payment; after 6 weeks, give the account to a collection agency and forget it. Focus <u>your</u> energy on growing your business, don't waste it chasing deadbeats.

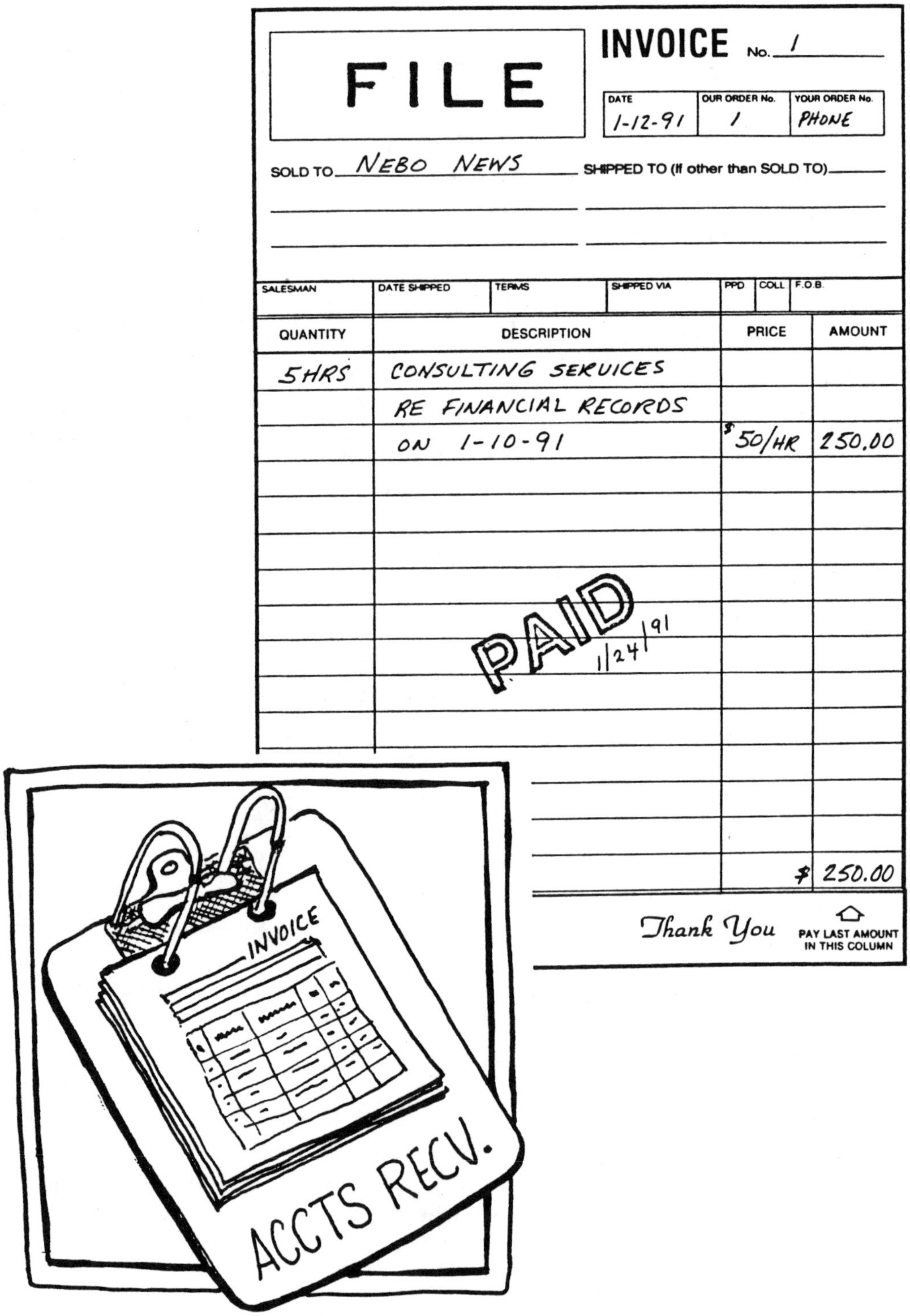

FIGURE 25 Accounts Receivable Invoice and Clipboard

Definition Of Business Expense Categories

Merchandise & Materials
Amounts paid for goods bought for resale. Goods may be finished products such as stock or inventory for retail sales or the raw materials that go into making, packaging & shipping the product to be sold. *(Note:* Businesses selling only services do not need this category).

Advertising
Amounts paid to promote your business, products and services. Includes advertising such as signs, yellow pages, newspaper, radio, and television; promotional gifts such as key rings, pens, calendars; direct mailings of flyers, brochures, and catalogs including amounts paid for postage and labor to prepare mailings.

Telephone
Amounts paid for use of telephone, answering services, and other telecommunications such as fax, modems, telegrams, and mailgrams.

Supplies
Amounts paid for items consumed in operating the business but which are not part of the product. Includes office supplies such as paper, pens, forms, stationery, postage, and general supplies such as binding materials, rags, twine and small hand tools under $200. *(Note:* If you have a mail order business, postage for product shipment should be included under Merchandise and Material).

Rents & Utilities
Amounts paid for use of someone else's property such as office space, buildings equipment, or machinery; utilities include amounts paid for electricity, water, heating fuels, refuse removal and janitorial work.

Maintenance & Repairs
Amounts paid for upkeep and repair of business property such as buildings, office equipment, and machinery other than autos. *(Note:* Repairs over $200 which lengthen the useful life or improve productive capacity of the equipment must be depreciated.

Insurance
Amounts paid to insure business against losses from accidents, fire, and legal liability, including workers' compensation. *(Note:* Medical and term life insurance premiums are Employee Benefits expenses, and premiums for auto insurance are included under Auto/Truck expenses).

Interest
Amounts paid for use of someone else's money. Includes interest and finance charges on loans, credit cards, bank advances and business accounts (may be entered either monthly or at end of year).

Contract Services
Amounts paid for services by non-employees such as word processing and typesetting, bookkeeping, accounting, legal, and other specialized assistance required by your business. This category also includes commissions paid to sales agents, temporary workers, and other contracted services. *(Note:* A non-employee

compensation Form 1099 must be submitted for each individual paid more than $600 during the course of the year).

Car/Truck   Amounts paid for operation, upkeep, and repair of autos and trucks used in the business; includes licenses, inspections, insurance, taxes, routine maintenance, tune-up/repairs, washing, gas, and oil. (*Note:* repairs over $200 that increase useful life such as new engine or new tires, must be depreciated).

Travel   Amounts paid for business travel including air, bus, and train fares, rental cars, parking, tolls, taxis, hotel or other lodging, laundry and dry cleaning, tips to porters, phone calls, haircuts, and other incidental expenses while away from home. (*Note:* commuting expenses are not considered travel and are not deductible).

Meals & Entertainment   Amounts paid for meals while on business trips and amounts paid to entertain customers, employees, business associates and prospects. (*Note:* business purpose must be documented and expenses are subject to IRS limitations).

Dues, Publications & Training   Amounts paid to keep up with the field or business. Includes dues, and subscriptions, tuition for training courses and memberships which contribute to maintaining and growing the business.

Refunds   Amounts paid for return of merchandise or refunded because of dissatisfaction.

Sales Tax   Amounts paid to state or local authorities for sales taxes you *collected*. (*Note:* This category is never used to record sales taxes paid, as such taxes are accounted for by recording total cost of purchases including sales tax).

State & Local Taxes   Amounts paid for property taxes on business real estate, equipment (other than vehicles) and inventory; also amounts paid for special licenses and state income tax and franchise fees on a corporation.

Bank Charges   Amounts paid for monthly service charges, check printing or special services such as returned checks and stop payments (a separate category for this item simplifies and speeds monthly balancing).

Miscellaneous   Amounts paid for incidental expenses such as small fees, contributions, gifts, and flowers.

Wages   This category includes amounts paid directly to employees. Since checks made out to employees are net of tax and other withholdings, it is simpler to use net figures in this category through the year and adjust to the "gross wage" figure (from payroll record) at the end of the year.

Payroll Taxes & Withholding   Amounts withheld from employees pay for income, Social Security and Medicare taxes and sent to government agencies on their behalf; also includes all employer paid payroll taxes such as employer's matching Social Security and Medicare taxes and federal (FUTA) and state unemployment taxes. Since both employee and employer taxes are paid on one check, it's easier to record both in this category through the year and determine employer payroll tax at end of year.

Employee Benefits   Amounts paid for such employee benefits as: health insurance premiums and reimbursements, child care services, financial or legal services, life or disability insurance premiums, contributions to savings plans, awards and other incentives.

Retirement Plans   Amounts paid to qualified retirement plans such as SEP-IRA, KEOGH, and pension plans.

Non-Deductible   Amounts paid to:

- owner - for any purpose (owner draws can also be shown as a separate line item);

- repay loan principal - because loans aren't taxable when the funds are received, repayments of loan principal are not deductible; (*interest* paid on loans is deductible and entered under Interest category);

- purchase depreciable assets such as furniture, fixtures, equipment, machinery, and other items which must be depreciated at end of year using IRS formulas.

- previously deducted purchases such as those included in previous year's accrual adjustments.

Finding Balance Errors

1. Examine the exact difference between the end of month bank balance and the closing balance on the Financial Summary (book balance). Does the figure look familiar? Is the amount of a check? A deposit? A bank charge or credit? An income or expense category total?

2. If the difference amount is not a familiar figure, begin by checking the last entries made on the Financial Summary. Was bank interest correctly entered under interest income? Were all bank service charges correctly entered under bank expense? Make sure you've included any unusual charges to your account—for returned checks or check printing, for example. Check your adding machine tape for reversed numbers; that is instead of entering 15.10, you entered 10.15 or 51.10 by mistake.

3. If all figures on the Financial Summary were entered correctly, see if the total income on the Financial Summary equals the total bank deposits (those appearing on the statement plus any you've added in the adjustment on the reverse side). If amounts agree, the error lies in the outstanding checks figure.

4. Make sure your check record accurately shows which checks have already cleared the bank. If your bank statement lists checks in numerical order, use the statement as a guide for marking your check record (see 5 below). If your bank doesn't list checks in numerical order, you have to arrange the canceled checks in numerical order and then use them as a guide to mark your check record.

5. Examine your check record to be sure all outstanding checks have been listed in your bank balance computation; it's easy to overlook those that haven't cleared from a previous month. The recommended procedure is to put a check mark (✓) in your checkbook to show a check has cleared. So any check entry without a (✓) mark means it is still outstanding. Of course, it's possible you forgot to make the check mark (✓) for a check that has already cleared, so if you've still not found the error, make sure all entries without a (✓) are really still outstanding. You may have too look at the previous statement to make certain the check hadn't cleared earlier and you just forgot to check it off. When looking for the error, concentrate on the amounts as well as the check number because often the computer doesn't pick up the number and simply lists the amount of the check. Some statements list them as an "unnumbered item"—still they are easy to miss when you're checking off your records.

6. If these inspections fail to turn up the difficulty, it may be a bank error. First, make sure the bank statement's beginning balance is the same as last month's statement's ending balance. Next, look for a possible key punch error by comparing each canceled check to see

if the computer entered amount is the same as the amount you wrote (see Figure 26). Note how statements listing checks in numerical order save time by eliminating need to arrange canceled checks in numerical order or having to examine individual checks for correct key punching.

7. No success? Try putting the material away for a few hours (or a few days!) and repeat the process when you're fresh.

8. If you still can't find the error, just assume *you* made the mistake and adjust your Financial Summary so it agrees with the bank balance computation. Say the ending balance on the Financial Summary is $2.50 low: simply add $2.50 to Other Income on the Summary. If the ending balance was $2.50 high: add $2.50 to "Bank Charges". Explain the adjustment on the back of the Financial Summary form: "Other Income" increased $2.50 to agree with ending bank balance." Normally, any adjustment will be small. If it isn't, ask your bank to help you locate the mistake.

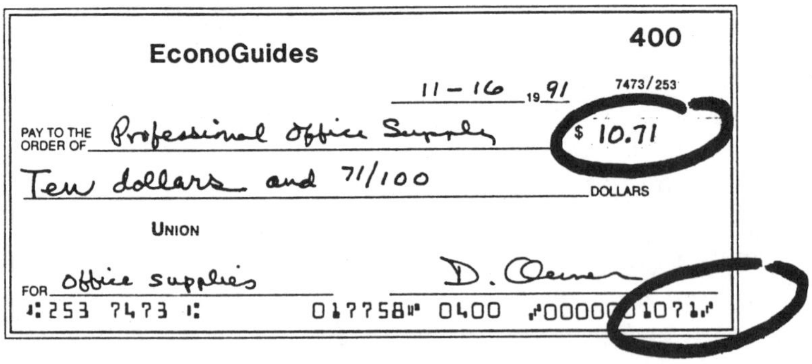

FIGURE 26 Looking For Bank's Key Punch Error

Calculating Depreciation

The tables in Figure 27 can be used to determine the annual depreciation of common business property; here's how:

1. Select method of depreciation. Note the Declining Balance method may be used only if property is used more than 50% for business.

2. Multiply purchase price by the percentage figure shown to determine the amount of depreciation for a given year. (For example, first year depreciation on a $4,000 truck using straight line method = $400; using the 200% declining balance = $800. Second year depreciation is $800 using straight line and $1,280 declining balance.

3. If property is not used 100% for business, depreciation must be reduced. (For example, if use of truck was 80% business, then the depreciation would be 80% of the indicated depreciation—$320, rather than $400 for the first year using straight line, and $640 instead of $800 using declining balance).

4. The above tables *cannot* be used if more than 40% of property put into service in a given year was acquired in the last 3 months of the year. In that case, mid-quarter rather than half-year rules would apply.

eg *The owner decided to expense half of the $4,000 truck cost under Section 179 Expensing, which leaves a depreciable value of $2,000. Choosing the 200% declining balance method results in a first year deduction of $400 (2,000 X 20%), bringing the total first year deduction to $2,400 ($2,000 expensing plus $400 depreciation) which is within the $2,660 limitation on first year deduction for vehicles in 1991 (see Figure 28 for required depreciation record).*

PROPERTY	DATE	COST	179 DEDUCTION	BALANCE TO DEPREC.	DEPREC.	TOTAL DEPREC.	BALANCE FORWARD
OFFICE EQUIP	1-91	235	235	0		235	0
TRUCK	6-91	4,000	2,000	2,000	400 (2DB)	2400	1,600
COMPUTER	12-91	1,000	1,000	0		1000	0
TOTAL	1991	5,235	3,235	2,000	400	3,635	1,600
	1992						
TRUCK	6-91	4,000		1,600	640 (2DB)	3,040	960

FIGURE 28 Depreciation Record

Five Year Property: Autos, light trucks, computers, typewriters, copiers, construction equipment

YEAR	STRAIGHT LINE	200% DECLINING BALANCE
1	10%	20.00%
2	20	32.00
3	20	19.20
4	20	11.52
5	20	11.52
6	10	5.76

Seven Year Property: Office furniture, fixtures, single purpose agricultural structures, and property not assigned to another class.

YEAR	STRAIGHT LINE	200% DECLINING BALANCE
1	7.13%	14.29%
2	14.29	24.49
3	14.29	17.49
4	14.29	12.49
5	14.29	8.93
6	14.29	8.93
7	14.29	8.93
8	7.13	4.45

FIGURE 27 Depreciation Tables Using Half-Year Convention

Tax Returns

Schedule C Calculations

Cost Of Goods Sold   The tax rules say that only the cost of the goods *actually* sold during the year can be deducted as an expense. For non-manufacturing businesses, like EconoGuides, the calculation is simple:

Inventory at beginning of year	$ 0
Plus inventory bought during year	3600
Inventory at end of the year	340
Cost of goods sold	$ 3260

In manufacturing businesses the cost of goods sold must also include the labor, facilities and other costs involved in manufacturing the product. This calculation can be quite complicated and usually requires the assistance of a preparer.

Income & Expense Entries   The income and expense *totals* on the Schedule C will differ from those on the Financial Summary because Merchandise and Refund *expenses* are accounted for in the *income* portion of Schedule C as cost of goods sold and returns and allowances (Figure 29).

Notice that gross wages ($480) are entered under "wages" and employer paid payroll taxes ($55) are entered under "taxes and licenses."

Net Profit   Note that the net profit on the Financial Summary is exactly the same as that on the Schedule C ($1,005), and how the figure is used on line 12 of the 1040 form and line 2 on Schedule SE to compute taxes due.

SCHEDULE C (Form 1040)

Department of the Treasury
Internal Revenue Service (X)

Profit or Loss From Business
(Sole Proprietorship)

▶ Partnerships, joint ventures, etc., must file Form 1065.

▶ Attach to Form 1040 or Form 1041. ▶ See Instructions for Schedule C (Form 1040).

OMB No. 1545-0074

1991

Attachment Sequence No. 09

Name of proprietor | **Social security number (SSN)**

A Principal business or profession, including product or service (see instructions)

B Enter principal business code (from page 2) ▶ 7 6 5 8

C Business name | **D** Employer ID number (Not SSN)

E Business address (including suite or room no.) ▶ ....
City, town or post office, state, and ZIP code

F Accounting method: (1) ☐ Cash (2) ☐ Accrual (3) ☑ Other (specify) ▶ MODIFIED ACCRUAL

G Method(s) used to value closing inventory: (1) ☑ Cost (2) ☐ Lower of cost or market (3) ☐ Other (attach explanation) (4) ☐ Does not apply (if checked, skip line H) | Yes | No

H Was there any change in determining quantities, costs, or valuations between opening and closing inventory? (If "Yes," attach explanation.) | | ☑

I Did you "materially participate" in the operation of this business during 1991? (If "No," see instructions for limitations on losses.) | ☑ |

J If this is the first Schedule C filed for this business, check here ▶ ☑

Part I Income

1	Gross receipts or sales. **Caution:** If this income was reported to you on Form W-2 and the "Statutory employee" box on that form was checked, see the instructions and check here ▶ ☐	1	10,860
2	Returns and allowances	2	63
3	Subtract line 2 from line 1	3	10,797
4	Cost of goods sold (from line 40 on page 2)	4	3,260
5	Subtract line 4 from line 3 and enter the **gross profit** here	5	7,537
6	Other income, including Federal and state gasoline or fuel tax credit or refund (see instructions)	6	7,380
7	Add lines 5 and 6. This is your **gross income** ▶	7	14,917

Part II Expenses (Caution: Enter expenses for business use of your home on line 30.)

8	Advertising	8	2,308	21 Repairs and maintenance	21	48
9	Bad debts from sales or services (see instructions)	9		22 Supplies (not included in Part III)	22	924
10	Car and truck expenses (see instructions—also attach Form 4562)	10	1,344	23 Taxes and licenses	23	55
11	Commissions and fees	11		24 Travel, meals, and entertainment:		
12	Depletion	12		a Travel	24a	568
13	Depreciation and section 179 expense deduction (not included in Part III) (see instructions)	13	3,635	b Meals and entertainment 675		
				c Enter 20% of line 24b subject to limitations (see instructions) 135		
14	Employee benefit programs (other than on line 19)	14		d Subtract line 24c from line 24b	24d	540
15	Insurance (other than health)	15	120	25 Utilities	25	682
16	Interest:			26 Wages (less jobs credit)	26	480
a	Mortgage (paid to banks, etc.)	16a		27a Other expenses (list type and amount):		
b	Other	16b	180	DUES/PUB 348		
17	Legal and professional services	17	690	BANK CHGS 42		
18	Office expense	18		MISCL 99		
19	Pension and profit-sharing plans	19				
20	Rent or lease (see instructions):					
a	Vehicles, machinery, and equipment	20a				
b	Other business property	20b		27b Total other expenses	27b	489

28	Add amounts in columns for lines 8 through 27b. These are your **total expenses** before expenses for business use of your home ▶	28	12,063
29	Tentative profit (loss). Subtract line 28 from line 7	29	2,854
30	Expenses for business use of your home (attach **Form 8829**)	30	1,849
31	**Net profit or (loss).** Subtract line 30 from line 29. If a profit, enter here and on Form 1040, line 12. Also enter the net profit on Schedule SE, line 2 (statutory employees, see instructions). If a loss, you MUST go on to line 32 (fiduciaries, see instructions)	31	1,005
32	If you have a loss, you MUST check the box that describes your investment in this activity (see instructions)	32a ☐ All investment is at risk	
	If you checked 32a, enter the loss on Form 1040, line 12, and Schedule SE, line 2 (statutory employees, see instructions). If you checked 32b, you MUST attach **Form 6198.**	32b ☐ Some investment is not at risk	

Part III Cost of Goods Sold (See instructions.)

33	Inventory at beginning of year. (If different from last year's closing inventory, attach explanation.)	33	0
34	Purchases less cost of items withdrawn for personal use	34	3,600
35	Cost of labor. (Do not include salary paid to yourself.)	35	
36	Materials and supplies	36	
37	Other costs	37	
38	Add lines 33 through 37	38	
39	Inventory at end of year	39	340
40	**Cost of goods sold.** Subtract line 39 from line 38. Enter the result here and on page 1, line 4	40	3,260

FIGURE 29 The Schedule C

Form 4562 — Depreciation and Amortization (Including Information on Listed Property)

Department of the Treasury — Internal Revenue Service
OMB No. 1545-0172
1991
Attachment Sequence No. 67

▶ See separate instructions. ▶ Attach this form to your return.

Name(s) shown on return

Identifying number

Business or activity to which this form relates

Part I — Election To Expense Certain Tangible Property (Section 179) (Note: If you have any "Listed Property," complete Part V.)

1 Maximum dollar limitation (see instructions)	1	$10,000
2 Total cost of section 179 property placed in service during the tax year (see instructions)	2	5,000
3 Threshold cost of section 179 property before reduction in limitation	3	$200,000
4 Reduction in limitation—Subtract line 3 from line 2, but do not enter less than -0-	4	0
5 Dollar limitation for tax year—Subtract line 4 from line 1, but do not enter less than -0-	5	10,000

6 (a) Description of property	(b) Cost	(c) Elected cost
OFFICE EQUIPMENT	235	235
	3000	

7 Listed property—Enter amount from line 26	7	3000
8 Total elected cost of section 179 property—Add amounts in column (c), lines 6 and 7	8	3235
9 Tentative deduction—Enter the lesser of line 5 or line 8	9	3235
10 Carryover of disallowed deduction from 1990 (see instructions)	10	
11 Taxable income limitation—Enter the lesser of taxable income or line 5 (see instructions)	11	10,000
12 Section 179 expense deduction—Add lines 9 and 10, but do not enter more than line 11	12	3,235
13 Carryover of disallowed deduction to 1992—Add lines 9 and 10, less line 12 ▶ 13		

Note: Do not use Part II or Part III below for automobiles, certain other vehicles, cellular telephones, computers, or property used for entertainment, recreation, or amusement (listed property). Instead, use Part V for listed property.

Part II — MACRS Depreciation For Assets Placed in Service ONLY During Your 1991 Tax Year (Do Not Include Listed Property)

14 (a) Classification of property	(b) Mo. and yr. placed in service	(c) Basis for depreciation (Business/investment use only—see instructions)	(d) Recovery period	(e) Convention	(f) Method	(g) Depreciation deduction
a 3-year property						
b 5-year property						
c 7-year property						
d 10-year property						
e 15-year property						
f 20-year property						
g Residential rental property			27.5 yrs.	MM	S/L	
			27.5 yrs.	MM	S/L	
h Nonresidential real property			31.5 yrs.	MM	S/L	
			31.5 yrs.	MM	S/L	

Part III — Alternative Depreciation System (ADS) (see instructions):

15						
a Class life					S/L	
b 12-year			12 yrs.		S/L	
c 40-year			40 yrs.	MM	S/L	

Part III — Other Depreciation (Do Not Include Listed Property)

16 GDS and ADS deductions for assets placed in service in tax years beginning before 1991 (see instructions)	16	
17 Property subject to section 168(f)(1) election (see instructions)	17	
18 ACRS and other depreciation (see instructions)	18	

Part IV — Summary

19 Listed property—Enter amount from line 25	19	400
20 Total—Add deductions on line 12, lines 14 and 15 in column (g), and lines 16 through 19. Enter here and on the appropriate lines of your return. (Partnerships and S corporations—see instructions)	20	3635
21 For assets shown above and placed in service during the current year, enter the portion of the basis attributable to section 263A costs (see instructions)	21	

For Paperwork Reduction Act Notice, see page 1 of the separate instructions. Cat. No. 12906N Form 4562 (1991)

Form 4562 (1991) — Page 2

Part V — Listed Property.—Automobiles, Certain Other Vehicles, Cellular Telephones, Computers, and Property Used for Entertainment, Recreation, or Amusement

If you are using the standard mileage rate or deducting vehicle lease expense, complete columns (a) through (c) of Section A, all of Section B, and Section C if applicable.

Section A.—Depreciation (Caution: See instructions for limitations for automobiles.)

22a Do you have evidence to support the business/investment use claimed? ☐ Yes ☐ No 22b If "Yes," is the evidence written? ☐ Yes ☐ No

23 (a) Type of property (list vehicles first)	(b) Date placed in service	(c) Business/ investment use percentage	(d) Cost or other basis	(e) Basis for depreciation (business/investment use only)	(f) Recovery period	(g) Method/ Convention	(h) Depreciation deduction	(i) Elected section 179 cost
Property used more than 50% in a qualified business use (see instructions):								
LIGHT TRUCK	6-10-91	100%	4000	2000	5	DB	400	2000
COMPUTER	12-1-91	100%	1000	1000	5	DB		1000
		%						
24 Property used 50% or less in a qualified business use (see instructions):								
		%			S/L –			
		%			S/L –			

25 Add amounts in column (h). Enter the total here and on line 19, page 1	25	400
26 Add amounts in column (i). Enter the total here and on line 7, page 1	26	3000

Section B.—Information Regarding Use of Vehicles—If you deduct expenses for vehicles:

• Always complete this section for vehicles used by a sole proprietor, partner, or other "more than 5% owner," or related person.
• If you provided vehicles to your employees, first answer the questions in Section C to see if you meet an exception to completing this section for those vehicles.

	(a) Vehicle 1		(b) Vehicle 2		(c) Vehicle 3		(d) Vehicle 4		(e) Vehicle 5		(f) Vehicle 6	
27 Total business/investment miles driven during the year (DO NOT include commuting miles)	4876		2925									
28 Total commuting miles driven during the year			3485									
29 Total other personal (noncommuting) miles driven			5708									
30 Total miles driven during the year—Add lines 27 through 29	4876		12118									
	Yes	No	Yes	No	Yes	No	Yes	No	Yes	No	Yes	No
31 Was the vehicle available for personal use during off-duty hours?		✓		✓								
32 Was the vehicle used primarily by a more than 5% owner or related person?		✓		✓								
33 Is another vehicle available for personal use?		✓		✓								

Section C.—Questions for Employers Who Provide Vehicles for Use by Their Employees

(Answer these questions to determine if you meet an exception to completing Section B. Note: Section B must always be completed for vehicles used by sole proprietors, partners, or other more than 5% owners or related persons.)

	Yes	No
34 Do you maintain a written policy statement that prohibits all personal use of vehicles, including commuting, by your employees?		
35 Do you maintain a written policy statement that prohibits personal use of vehicles, except commuting, by your employees? (See instructions for vehicles used by corporate officers, directors, or 1% or more owners)		
36 Do you treat all use of vehicles by employees as personal use?		
37 Do you provide more than five vehicles to your employees and retain the information received from your employees concerning the use of the vehicles?		
38 Do you meet the requirements concerning qualified automobile demonstration use (see instructions)?		

Note: If your answer to 34, 35, 36, 37, or 38 is "Yes," you need not complete Section B for the covered vehicles.

Part VI — Amortization

39 (a) Description of costs	(b) Date amortization begins	(c) Amortizable amount	(d) Code section	(e) Amortization period or percentage	(f) Amortization for this year
Amortization of costs that begins during your 1991 tax year:					

40 Amortization of costs that began before 1991	40	
41 Total. Enter here and on "Other Deductions" or "Other Expenses" line of your return	41	

Form 4562 (1991)

FIGURE 30 Form 4562 Depreciation & Automobile Use

Form **8829**	**Expenses for Business Use of Your Home**	OMB No. 1545-1256
Department of the Treasury Internal Revenue Service	▶ File with Schedule C (Form 1040). ▶ See Instructions on back.	**1991** Attachment Sequence No. 66
Name of proprietor		Your social security number

Part I   Part of Your Home Used for Business

1	Area used exclusively for business (see instructions). Include area used for inventory storage or as a day-care facility that does not meet exclusive use test	1	300
2	Total area of home	2	2000
3	Divide line 1 by line 2. Enter the result as a percentage	3	15 %

- For day-care facilities not used exclusively for business, also complete lines 4–6.
- All others, skip lines 4–6 and enter the amount from line 3 on line 7.

4	Total hours facility used for day care during the year. Multiply days used by number of hours used per day	4	hr.
5	Total hours available for use during the year (365 days x 24 hours) (see instructions)	5	8,760 hr.
6	Divide line 4 by line 5. Enter the result as a decimal amount	6	.
7	Business percentage. For day-care facilities not used exclusively for business, multiply line 6 by line 3 (enter the result as a percentage). All others, enter the amount from line 3 ▶	7	15 %

Part II   Figure Your Allowable Deduction

		(a) Direct expenses	(b) Indirect expenses		
8	Enter the amount from Schedule C, line 29. (If more than one place of business, see instructions.)			8	2854
9	Casualty losses				
10	Deductible mortgage interest		7200		
11	Real estate taxes		800		
12	Add lines 9, 10, and 11		8000		
13	Multiply line 12, column (b) by line 7		1200		
14	Add line 12, column (a) and line 13			14	1200
15	Subtract line 14 from line 8. If zero or less, enter -0-			15	1654
16	Excess mortgage interest (see instructions)				
17	Insurance		400		
18	Repairs and maintenance		500		
19	Utilities		1600		
20	Other expenses				
21	Add lines 16 through 20		2500		
22	Multiply line 21, column (b) by line 7	375			
23	Carryover of operating expenses from 1990				
24	Add line 21 in column (a), line 22, and line 23			24	375
25	Allowable operating expenses. Enter the smaller of line 15 or line 24			25	375
26	Limit on excess casualty losses and depreciation. Subtract line 25 from line 15			26	1279
27	Excess casualty losses (see instructions)				
28	Depreciation of your home from Part III below	274			
29	Carryover of excess casualty losses and depreciation from 1990				
30	Add lines 27 through 29			30	274
31	Allowable excess casualty losses and depreciation. Enter the smaller of line 26 or line 30			31	274
32	Add lines 14, 25, and 31			32	1849
33	Casualty losses included on lines 14 and 31. (Carry this amount to Form 4684, Section B.)			33	
34	Allowable expenses for business use of your home. Subtract line 33 from line 32. Enter here and on Schedule C, line 30 ▶			34	1849

Part III   Depreciation of Your Home

35	Enter the smaller of your home's adjusted basis or its fair market value (see instructions)	35	70,000
36	Value of land included on line 35	36	10,000
37	Basis of building. Subtract line 36 from line 35	37	60,000
38	Business basis of building. Multiply line 37 by line 7	38	9,000
39	Depreciation percentage (see instructions)	39	3.042 %
40	Depreciation allowable. Multiply line 38 by the percentage on line 39. Enter here and on line 28 above	40	274

Part IV   Carryover of Unallowed Expenses to 1992

41	Operating expenses. Subtract line 25 from line 24. If less than zero, enter -0-	41	
42	Excess casualty losses and depreciation. Subtract line 31 from line 30. If less than zero, enter -0-	42	

FIGURE 31   Form 8829 Business Use Of Home

SCHEDULE SE (Form 1040) Department of the Treasury Internal Revenue Service (M)	Self-Employment Tax ▶ See Instructions for Schedule SE (Form 1040). ▶ Attach to Form 1040.	OMB No. 1545-0074 19**91** Attachment Sequence No. **17**

Name of person with **self-employment** income (as shown on Form 1040)	Social security number of person with **self-employment** income ▶	

Who Must File Schedule SE

You must file Schedule SE if:

- Your *net earnings from self-employment from other than church employee income* (line 4 of Short Schedule SE or line 4c of Long Schedule SE) were $400 or more; **OR**
- You had church employee income (as defined in the instructions) of $108.28 or more;

    AND

- Your wages (and tips) subject to social security AND Medicare tax (or railroad retirement tax) were less than $125,000.

Exception: If your only self-employment income was from earnings as a minister, member of a religious order, or Christian Science practitioner, AND you filed **Form 4361** and received IRS approval not to be taxed on those earnings, DO NOT file Schedule SE. Instead, write "Exempt–Form 4361" on Form 1040, line 47.

Note: *Most people can use Short Schedule SE on this page. But you may have to use Long Schedule SE on the back.*

Who MUST Use Long Schedule SE (Section B)

You must use Long Schedule SE if ANY of the following apply:

- You received wages or tips **and** the total of all of your wages (and tips) subject to social security, Medicare, or railroad retirement tax plus your net earnings from self-employment is more than $53,400;
- You use either "optional method" to figure your net earnings from self-employment (see Section B, Part II, and the instructions);
- You are a minister, member of a religious order, or Christian Science practitioner and you received IRS approval (by filing Form 4361) not to be taxed on your earnings from these sources, but you owe self-employment tax on other earnings;
- You had church employee income of $108.28 or more that was reported to you on Form W-2; **OR**
- You received tips subject to social security, Medicare, or railroad retirement tax, but you did not report those tips to your employer.

Section A—Short Schedule SE (Read above to see if you must use Long Schedule SE on the back (Section B).)

1	Net farm profit or (loss) from Schedule F (Form 1040), line 37, and farm partnerships, Schedule K-1 (Form 1065), line 15a	1	
2	Net profit or (loss) from Schedule C (Form 1040), line 31, and Schedule K-1 (Form 1065), line 15a (other than farming). See instructions for other income to report	2	*1,005*
3	Combine lines 1 and 2	3	*1,005*
4	**Net earnings from self-employment.** Multiply line 3 by .9235. If less than $400, **do not** file this schedule; you **do not** owe self-employment tax. **Caution:** *If you received wages or tips, and the total of your wages (and tips) subject to social security, Medicare, or railroad retirement tax plus the amount on line 4 is more than $53,400, you cannot use Short Schedule SE. Instead, use Long Schedule SE on the back* . . . . ▶	4	*928*
5	**Self-employment tax.** If the amount on line 4 is: • $53,400 or less, multiply line 4 by 15.3% (.153) and enter the result. • More than $53,400, but less than $125,000, multiply the amount in excess of $53,400 by 2.9% (.029). Add $8,170.20 to the result and enter the total. • $125,000 or more, enter $10,246.60. Also enter this amount on Form 1040, line 47	5	*142*

Note: *Also enter one-half of the amount from line 5 on Form 1040, line 25.*

FIGURE 32 Schedule SE

Form 1040 (1991)   Page 2

Tax Computation

32	Amount from line 31 (adjusted gross income)	32	42,067
33a	Check if: You were 65 or older. ☐ Blind; Spouse was 65 or older ☐ Blind.		
b	Add the number of boxes checked above and enter the total here ▶ 33b ☐		
c	If your parent (or someone else) can claim you as a dependent, check here ▶ 33c ☐		

If you want the IRS to figure your tax, see page 24.

Itemized deductions (from Schedule A, line 26). **OR**

Standard deduction (shown below for your filing status). Caution: If you checked any box on line 33a or b, go to page 23 to find your standard deduction. If you checked box 33c, your standard deduction is zero.
● Single—$3,400 ● Married filing jointly or Qualifying widow(er)—$5,700 ● Head of household—$5,000 ● Married filing separately—$2,850

34	Enter the larger of your:	34	11,267
35	Subtract line 34 from line 32	35	30,800
36	If line 32 is $75,000 or less, multiply $2,150 by the total number of exemptions claimed on line 6e. If line 32 is over $75,000, see page 24 for the amount to enter	36	6,450
37	Taxable income. Subtract line 36 from line 35. (If line 36 is more than line 35, enter -0-.)	37	24,350
38	Enter tax. Check if from a ☑ Tax Table, b ☐ Tax Rate Schedules, c ☐ Schedule D, or d ☐ Form 8615 (see page 24). (Amount, if any, from Form(s) 8814 ▶ e)	38	3,656
39	Additional taxes (see page 24). Check if from a ☐ Form 4970 b ☐ Form 4972	39	
40	Add lines 38 and 39	40	3,656

Credits (See page 25.)

41	Credit for child and dependent care expenses (attach Form 2441)	41		
42	Credit for the elderly or the disabled (attach Schedule R)	42		
43	Foreign tax credit (attach Form 1116)	43		
44	Other credits (see page 25). Check if from a ☐ Form 3800 b ☐ Form 8396 c ☐ Form 8801 d ☐ Form (specify)	44		
45	Add lines 41 through 44	45		
46	Subtract line 45 from line 40. (If line 45 is more than line 40, enter -0-.)	46	3,656

Other Taxes

47	Self-employment tax (attach Schedule SE)	47	142
48	Alternative minimum tax (attach Form 6251)	48	
49	Recapture taxes (see page 26). Check if from a ☐ Form 4255 b ☐ Form 8611 c ☐ Form 8828	49	
50	Social security and Medicare tax on tip income not reported to employer (attach Form 4137)	50	
51	Tax on an IRA or a qualified retirement plan (attach Form 5329)	51	
52	Advance earned income credit payments from Form W-2	52	
53	Add lines 46 through 52. This is your **total tax** ▶	53	3,798

Payments — Attach Forms W-2, W-2G, and 1099-R to front.

54	Federal income tax withheld (if any is from Form(s) 1099 check ▶ ☐)	54	3,830
55	1991 estimated tax payments and amount applied from 1990 return	55	
56	Earned income credit (attach Schedule EIC)	56	
57	Amount paid with Form 4868 (extension request)	57	
58	Excess social security, Medicare and RRTA tax withheld (see page 27)	58	
59	Other payments (see page 27). Check if from a ☐ Form 2439 b ☐ Form 4136	59	
60	Add lines 54 through 59. These are your **total payments** ▶	60	3,830

Refund or Amount You Owe

61	If line 60 is more than line 53, subtract line 53 from line 60. This is the amount you **OVERPAID**	61	32
62	Amount of line 61 to be **REFUNDED TO YOU** ▶	62	32
63	Amount of line 61 to be **APPLIED TO YOUR 1992 ESTIMATED TAX** ▶ 63		
64	If line 53 is more than line 60, subtract line 60 from line 53. This is the **AMOUNT YOU OWE**. Attach check or money order for full amount payable to "Internal Revenue Service." Write your name, address, social security number, daytime phone number, and "1991 Form 1040" on it.	64	
65	Estimated tax penalty (see page 28). Also include on line 64.	65	

Sign Here — Keep a copy of this return for your records.

Under penalties of perjury, I declare that I have examined this return and accompanying schedules and statements, and to the best of my knowledge and belief, they are true, correct, and complete. Declaration of preparer (other than taxpayer) is based on all information of which preparer has any knowledge.

Your signature _____ Date _____ Your occupation _____
Spouse's signature (if joint return, BOTH must sign) _____ Date _____ Spouse's occupation _____

Paid Preparer's Use Only

Preparer's signature _____ Date _____ Check if self-employed ☐ Preparer's social security no. _____
Firm's name (or yours if self-employed) and address _____ E.I. No _____ ZIP code _____

Department of the Treasury—Internal Revenue Service
1040 U.S. Individual Income Tax Return 1991 (L)
For the year Jan.–Dec. 31, 1991, or other tax year beginning __, 1991, ending __, 19__   OMB No. 1545-0074

Label (See instructions on page 11.) Use the IRS label. Otherwise, please print or type.

Your first name and initial: OWNER   Last name   Your social security number
If a joint return, spouse's first name and initial   Last name   Spouse's social security number
Home address (number and street). (If you have a P.O. box, see page 11.)   Apt. no.
City, town or post office, state, and ZIP code. (If you have a foreign address, see page 11.)

For Privacy Act and Paperwork Reduction Act Notice, see instructions.

Presidential Election Campaign (See page 11.)
Do you want $1 to go to this fund?   Yes ☐   No ☐
If joint return, does your spouse want $1 to go to this fund?   Yes ☐   No ☐
Note: Checking "Yes" will not change your tax or reduce your refund.

Filing Status (Check only one box.)

1. ☑ Single
2. ☐ Married filing joint return (even if only one had income)
3. ☐ Married filing separate return. Enter spouse's social security no. above and full name here. ▶
4. ☐ Head of household (with qualifying person). (See page 12.) If the qualifying person is a child but not your dependent, enter this child's name here. ▶
5. ☐ Qualifying widow(er) with dependent child (year spouse died ▶ 19). (See page 12.)

Exemptions (See page 12.)

6a ☑ Yourself. If your parent (or someone else) can claim you as a dependent on his or her tax return, do not check box 6a. But be sure to check the box on line 33b on page 2.
b ☐ Spouse
c Dependents:

(1) Name (first, initial, and last name)	(2) Check if under age 1	(3) If age 1 or older, dependent's social security number	(4) Dependent's relationship to you	(5) No. of months lived in your home in 1991
ALEXANDRA			DAUGHTER	12

No. of boxes checked on 6a and 6b: **2**
No. of your children on 6c who: lived with you / didn't live with you due to divorce or separation (see page 13)
No. of other dependents on 6c: **1**
Add numbers entered on lines above ▶

d If your child didn't live with you but is claimed as your dependent under a pre-1985 agreement, check here ▶ ☐
e Total number of exemptions claimed

Income — Attach Copy B of your Forms W-2, W-2G, and 1099-R here. If you did not get a W-2, see page 10. Attach check or money order on top of any Forms W-2, W-2G, or 1099-R.

7	Wages, salaries, tips, etc. (attach Form(s) W-2)	7	43,500
8a	Taxable interest income (also attach Schedule B if over $400)	8a	514
b	Tax-exempt interest income (see page 16). DON'T include on line 8a	8b	
9	Dividend income (also attach Schedule B if over $400)	9	
10	Taxable refunds of state and local income taxes, if any, from worksheet on page 16	10	
11	Alimony received	11	1,005
12	Business income or (loss) (attach Schedule C)	12	
13	Capital gain or (loss) (attach Schedule D)	13	
14	Capital gain distributions not reported on line 13 (see page 17)	14	
15	Other gains or (losses) (attach Form 4797)	15	
16a	Total IRA distributions 16a	16b Taxable amount (see page 17)	16b	
17a	Total pensions and annuities 17a	17b Taxable amount (see page 17)	17b	
18	Rents, royalties, partnerships, estates, trusts, etc. (attach Schedule E)	18	
19	Farm income or (loss) (attach Schedule F)	19	
20	Unemployment compensation (insurance) (see page 18)	20	
21a	Social security benefits 21a	21b Taxable amount (see page 18)	21b	
22	Other income (list type and amount—see page 18)	22	
23	Add the amounts shown in the far right column for lines 7 through 22. This is your **total income** ▶	23	45,019

Adjustments to Income (See page 19.)

24a	Your IRA deduction, from applicable worksheet on page 20 or 21	24a	1,000
b	Spouse's IRA deduction, from applicable worksheet on page 20 or 21	24b	
25	One-half of self-employment tax (see page 22)	25	71
26	Self-employed health insurance deduction, from worksheet on page 22	26	750
27	Keogh retirement plan and self-employed SEP deduction	27	131
28	Penalty on early withdrawal of savings	28	
29	Alimony paid. Recipient's SSN ▶	29	
30	Add lines 24a through 29. These are your **total adjustments** ▶	30	2,952

Adjusted Gross Income

31	Subtract line 30 from line 23. This is your **adjusted gross income**. If this amount is less than $21,250 and a child lived with you, see page 45 to find out if you can claim the "Earned Income Credit" on line 56.	31	42,067

FIGURE 33 Individual Tax Return Form 1040

Retirement Plan Options

SEP-IRA Simplified Employee Pensions are, as the name implies, the simplest of plans. Each year, you are permitted to contribute 15% of <u>net</u> earnings from your business or $30,000, whichever is less, to a SEP-IRA. The rules say that the net earnings are the business profit *less the owner's contribution* to the SEP. In effect, that limits the maximum contribution of the owner to 13% of the profit rather than 15% that would apply to employees of the business. SEP-IRA plans may be opened and funded as late as April 15 of the following year. If the business has employees, a Salary Reduction SEP plans (SARSEP) should be considered. Under these plans, employees can elect to contribute up to 15% of their salaries up to a maximum of $8,475 (in 1991) to the plan rather than receiving the amount as salary. However, the combined employer and employee contribution to the plan still cannot exceed 15% of employee salary or $30,000 which ever is less.

KEOGH Named for the congressman who introduced the original legislation, these plans are also known as HR10 plans. They can take the form of either a *defined contribution* or a *defined benefit* plan.

Defined Contribution Plans:

Contributions to these plans are based on a percentage of the annual profits. There are three kinds of defined contribution plans:

■ Profit Sharing - allows *owner* to contribute up to 13% of profit or $30,000, whichever is less.

■ Money Purchase - Unlike Profit Sharing, this plan requires a *fixed percentage* of profit to be contributed each year. The fixed amount may range from 3% to 20%, but the total contribution is limited to $30,000 per year. In our example, the owner would be able to contribute a maximum of $201 (20% of the $1,005). However, this commits the owner to contributing 20% of his profit *every* year.

■ Paired Plans - Combines Profit Sharing with Money Purchase allowing the owner to combine a small fixed contribution with a variable one to gain flexibility. For example, many owners select a 7% money purchase contribution and contribute from 0 to 13% to profit sharing depending on how well they do each year. This way they can contribute the maximum allowable amount of 20% (or $30,000) in good years; and if they have better uses for the funds, they could reduce their retirement contribution to 7% of profits (the fixed money purchase percentage).

Defined Benefit Plans:

Contributions to defined benefit plans are determined by age and average salary, rather than annual profits. The older the owner and higher the salary, the more the owner can contribute. These plans are recommended for business owners over 45 years old, who have profitable businesses and want to contribute more than the limits imposed on defined contribution plans. A common defined benefit plan calls for an annual pension equal to 80% of the three highest earnings years. The annual contributions required by such plans can reduce the taxable business income to zero. The downside is that these plans involve a lot of paper work and are more costly to administer. In addition to filing Form 5500, a Schedule B must be completed by an actuary certifying the contribution calculations are correct. However, the additional time and expense is justified when the plan enables the owner to shelter more than otherwise possible.

If a Keogh plan covers only one person and the balance is less than $100,000, there are no reporting requirements (an owner and spouse can each have a single-person plan). However, if the plan has more than one person or if assets become greater than $100,000, the owner must file a form 5500 each year with the IRS. Keogh plans must be opened by *December 31.* Contributions to profit share plans may be made up until the following April 15, but contributions to money purchase plans must be made quarterly.

Regardless of the type of retirement plan selected, all full-time employees (over 1000 hours per year), *must* be included. If the employer decides to contribute the 15% maximum contribution for a SEP or KEOGH profit sharing plan in a given year, then 15% of each employee's salary that year must be contributed on their behalf. This is a deductible business expense and shown under Pension and Profit Sharing Plans on Schedule C. However, the *owner's* contribution would be limited to *13%* of the net profit; it would *not* be a deductible business expense, but would appear as a deduction on line 27 of the owner's 1040 return.

Employees acquire rights to contributions made in their behalf according to a *vesting schedule.* The rules call for full ownership (fully vested) by the end of 5 years if vesting occurs all at once, or by the end of 7 years if a more gradual vesting schedule is selected. Employees who leave the business may withdraw vested amounts, and must either pay income taxes on those amounts or redeposit them in another qualified retirement plan within 60 days.

Important! All money in Keogh and SEP plans compounds tax free until it is withdrawn, at which point it should be taxed at a lower rate. Keogh plans can be opened at most banks, brokerages and insurance companies. There is no limit on the number of Keogh plans opened, provided total contributions to the plans don't exceed the annual limits.

Employer Responsibilities

Hiring

Before adding anyone to your payroll, consider contracting for the service. Common contracted services are bookkeeping, typing and general secretarial work. Contracting for such services saves you the bother and expense of payroll taxes, records, and returns. The only reporting requirement for contracted services is to complete a Form 1099 Misc for each person paid over $600 during the year.

Make sure you contract with persons who offer their services to the general public, supply their own equipment, and are covered by their own worker's compensation policy. Otherwise, the IRS may regard the individual as your employee, making *you liable* for taxes, penalties, and interest on income the person failed to claim. You can avoid any questions by contracting with a temporary help or employee leasing agency, but it will cost more.

Adding someone to your payroll increases your legal liability. Many employers don't realize they can be sued for negligent acts of their employees. For example an *employer* was successfully sued when an employee backing out of the business driveway ran over a child. The employer may also be the target of an employee suit claiming injury or discrimination on the basis of age, sex, race, or other violation of civil rights. It's wise to have the following insurance coverage before placing anyone on the payroll:

- Business Owner's Policy - In addition to protecting against loss from fire and other hazards, these policies also protect you against loss from dishonest or irresponsible employees. Annual premiums usually under $300 per year.

- Workers' Compensation Policy - Workers' compensation is an inexpensive insurance that protects the owner from damage suits by employees should they become injured or incapacitated as a result of job-related activities. The premium depends on the number of employees and kind of work, beginning at about $300 per year.

Keep in mind that all of the owner's personal assets are at risk in an unincorporated business. This fact, combined with the added liabilities for the action or inactions of employees, make it advisable to reconsider the advantages of limited liability offered by the corporate form before becoming an employer.

Take time to do a thorough background and reference check on the employee candidates. Be patient. It may be better to have no one, rather than the wrong person when you're building a business. Plan on spending time observing and evaluating during a beginning probationary period. If the person isn't right for the job, have the courage to say so. This is especially difficult when it's a close friend or relative.

Employment practices that will keep you out of trouble include:

- written descriptions of the duties, responsibilities and performance expectations for each position.
- written performance evaluations at least once a year (read and signed by the employee).
- signed agreements where employee agrees to keep business information confidential, and acknowledges that outgrowths of work the employee has been paid to do, belong to the employer.
- signed and documented requests from employees for reimbursement for out-of-pocket expenses.

Important! State employment agencies frequently allow a probationary period for employees they refer. If probationary employees are let go, unemployment benefits are not charged against the company's account.

Employer Tax Forms & Returns

- *Form SS-4:* This is an application for a Federal ID number required of all employers. The Federal ID number will be required on all forms you send to the IRS and Social Security Administration. When your number is issued, you'll be put on a mailing list and sent all the necessary Federal payroll forms in time for filing. The SS-4 form is available from any IRS or Social Security office (check with your state agency for equivalent state form).

- *Form I-9:* This is a U.S. Immigration form you use to verify that the employee is legally eligible to work in the United States. You indicate which documents were used to verify citizenship or eligibility and keep the completed form in the employee's file. You can be fined if a completed I-9 form is not on file for each employee hired after 1986.

- *Form W-4:* This form is completed by the employee stating the number of withholding allowances the employee is claiming. You use this information to determine how much income tax to withhold from each paycheck. The form is kept in the employee's file, and remains in effect until the employee gives you a new one. Low income employees may be eligible for Earned Income Credit. Eligible employees may either take this credit on their income tax returns, or be paid the appropriate amount each pay period. If they choose the latter, they must complete a Form W-5 which is also kept in their file.

- *Form W-5:* This is an Earned Income Credit (EIC) Advanced Payment Certificate filed by employees who have a qualifying child and an adjusted gross income less than $21,250 (in 1991). The advanced EIC payments are provided for in each paycheck, generally through reductions in amounts withheld from income, Social Security and Medicare taxes.

- *Individual Payroll Record:* An individual payroll record is required to meet federal wage and hour regulations and protects the employer from claims of under payment. (See Figure 34).

At the end of each month columns are totaled to see if withholding taxes must be deposited. For federal taxes, if the amount owed is less than $500 at the end of any month, the deposit can be made with the quarterly return, Form 941 (Figure 35). Note that the federal deposit is equal to the taxes withheld plus *twice* the Social Security and Medicare taxes because the employer must match the employee contributions (36.00 + 2 X 36.72 = 109.44). Since the amount owed was less than $500, no deposit is required before filing the quarterly return. When the total is more than $500 a deposit using Form 8109 (Figure 36) is needed and reported in the space provided on the lower portion of the Quarterly Return (Form 941). Note that the employer is required to deduct 20% from wages as "backup withholding" for any employees awaiting a social security number.

The owner's daughter Alexandra is paid $6.00 per hour 20 hours each week for a gross weekly pay of $120. The federal withholding tax table (in Circular E, sent to each employer each year) for "Single Persons - Weekly Payroll Period" shows the tax for "1" withholding allowance (W-4 form) is $9.00 and is entered in the FWT column (Federal Withholding Tax). Social Security tax is $7.44 and Medicare tax is $1.74 (6.20% and 1.45% for 1991). The state also has an income tax and state tables indicate the amount to be withheld for state tax (SWT) is $1.57. The net pay is simply gross salary less all the withholdings ($100.25), and is the amount of the payroll check written to the employee.

- *Form 941:* This return must be filed at the end of each quarter (Figure 35). Note that the 12.4 % Social Security and 2.9% Medicare payments total 15.3% and represent both the employee and employer share of these taxes (7.65% *each for 1991*).

- *Form 8109:* Soon after you file for your Federal ID number, you will receive a booklet of these pre-printed coupons to be used in making your federal payroll tax deposits. Deposits may be made at any authorized depositaries—that is, most local banks. All you need do is give the coupon with the check to the bank on or before the date it is due. It's a good idea to put your Federal ID#, type of tax, and period covered on your check in case it gets separated from the coupon—it's been known to happen. And make sure the correct tax and period is marked on the coupon since this form is used to pay a number of different taxes (see Figure 36).

- *State Withholding Deposits:* States with income taxes will send you pre-printed coupons or forms for depositing taxes. Payments are usually made directly to the state.

PAYROLL RECORD: ALEXANDRA   SAL: 6.00/HR   W-4: 1

WK. ENDING	REG / OT	GROSS PAY	FWT	SS	MED	SWT	NET PAY
12-6-91	20/0	120.00	9.00	7.44	1.74	1.57	100.25
12-13-91	20/0	120.00	9.00	7.44	1.74	1.57	100.25
12-20-91	20/0	120.00	9.00	7.44	1.74	1.57	100.25
12-27-91	20/0	120.00	9.00	7.44	1.74	1.57	100.25
TOTAL DECEMBER	80/0	480.00	36.00	29.76	6.96	6.28	401.00
TOTAL 4TH QTR	80/0	480.00	36.00	29.76	6.96	6.28	401.00

SINGLE Persons–WEEKLY Payroll Period
(For Wages Paid After December 1990)

And the wages are–		And the number of withholding allowances claimed is–										
At least	But less than	0	1	2	3	4	5	6	7	8	9	10
		The amount of income tax to be withheld shall be–										
95	100	11	5	0	0	0	0	0	0	0	0	0
100	105	12	6	0	0	0	0	0	0	0	0	0
105	110	13	6	0	0	0	0	0	0	0	0	0
110	115	13	7	1	0	0	0	0	0	0	0	0
115	120	14	8	2	0	0	0	0	0	0	0	0
120	125	15	9	2	0	0	0	0	0	0	0	0
125	130	16	9	3	0	0	0	0	0	0	0	0
130	135	16	10	4	0	0	0	0	0	0	0	0
135	140	17	11	5	0	0	0	0	0	0	0	0
140	145	18	12	5	0	0	0	0	0	0	0	0

FIGURE 34 Individual Payroll Record & FWT Table

Late penalties can be severe, 25% of the tax plus interest, so it pays to send in payments and returns on time.

- **Unemployment Taxes:** In addition to paying social security taxes, the employer must pay federal and, usually, state unemployment taxes. When state unemployment taxes are payable, the federal unemployment tax (FUTA) is .008 of the first $7,000 of each employee's income. The tax is payable within 30 days of the end of each quarter using Form 8109 (Figure 36). At the end of the year, a FUTA tax return (Form 940) must be filed with any balance due (Figure 37). Note that unemployment taxes are paid *entirely* by the employer.

  State unemployment taxes are usually filed and payable on a quarterly basis. Initial rates are usually between 3% and 5% of some specified earnings limit. When a sufficient balance is reached and no unemployment claims have been made, the rate can drop to 1% or less. State unemployment offices generally send forms or coupons for making payments.

The Federal Unemployment (FUTA) tax was $3.84 (480 x .008). The amount paid for State unemployment was a fraction over 3%, $14.44. Note that the amount paid into state unemployment insurance is shown on the federal (FUTA) return.

- **Form W-2:** This familiar form is completed annually by the employer and shows the total amount of wages, income taxes withheld and Social Security and Medicare taxes paid (Figure 38). The W-2 provides a space for state income taxes withheld and can be used by the employee for filing state taxes as well. The W-2 must be given or mailed to each employee prior to January 31 of the following year. All the information needed to prepare the W-2 is found on the employee's payroll record. Copies of all W-2 forms must be sent with a transmittal form (W-3) to the Social Security Administration before February 28 of following year (Figure 38).

- **Form 1099:** You must complete a form 1099 Misc (Figure 39) for each person paid more than $600 for services or rents during the year. Forms must be sent to the individuals prior to January 31 of the following year, with copies transmitted to the IRS by February 28 on transmittal form 1096 (Figure 39).

Important! If you have several employees and want no part of keeping up with all these payroll records (and who could blame you?), consider using a local bank or payroll service. The annual cost for processing the payroll for 3 to 4 employees currently ranges from $500 to $1000, depending on where you live, and includes: maintaining records, issuing checks and earnings statements, filing federal and state tax returns, preparing tax deposits, and providing annual W-2, and 1099 statements.

Form **941**		**Employer's Quarterly Federal Tax Return**		
(Rev. January 1991) Department of the Treasury Internal Revenue Service	4141	▶ See Circular E for more information concerning employment tax returns. **Please type or print.**		

Type or print your name, address, employer identification number, and calendar quarter of return as shown on original. ▶

Name (as distinguished from trade name)	Date quarter ended	OMB No 1545-0029 Expires 5-31-93
Trade name, if any	Employer identification number	
Address and ZIP code		

If you do not have to file returns in the future, check here . . ▶ ☐   Date final wages paid . . . ▶ _____

If you are a seasonal employer, see **Seasonal employers** on page 2 and check here . . ▶ ☐

1a	Number of employees (except household) employed in the pay period that includes March 12th ▶	**1a**		
b	If you are a subsidiary corporation AND your parent corporation files a consolidated Form 1120, enter parent corporation employer identification number (EIN) . ▶ **1b** —			
2	Total wages and tips subject to withholding, plus other compensation . . . . ▶	**2**	480	00
3	Total income tax withheld from wages, tips, pensions, annuities, sick pay, gambling, etc. . ▶	**3**	36	00
4	Adjustment of withheld income tax for preceding quarters of calendar year (see instructions) . ▶	**4**		
5	Adjusted total of income tax withheld (line 3 as adjusted by line 4—see instructions)	**5**	36	00
6a	Taxable social security wages **(Complete line 7)** $ 480 00 × 12.4% (.124) =	**6a**	59	52
b	Taxable social security tips $ × 12.4% (.124) =	**6b**		
7	Taxable Medicare wages and tips . . . . . $ 480 00 × 2.9% (.029) =	**7**	13	92
8	Total social security and Medicare taxes (add lines 6a, 6b, and 7)	**8**	73	44
9	Adjustment of social security and Medicare taxes (see instructions for required explanation) . . .	**9**		
10	Adjusted total of social security and Medicare taxes (line 8 as adjusted by line 9—see instructions) ▶	**10**	73	44
11	Backup withholding (see instructions)	**11**		
12	Adjustment of backup withholding tax for preceding quarters of calendar year. . . . . . ▶	**12**		
13	Adjusted total of backup withholding (line 11 as adjusted by line 12)	**13**		
14	**Total taxes** (add lines 5, 10, and 13)	**14**	109	44
15	Advance earned income credit (EIC) payments made to employees, if any . . . . . . ▶	**15**		
16	Net taxes (subtract line 15 from line 14). **This should equal line IV below** (plus line IV of Schedule A (Form 941) if you have treated backup withholding as a separate liability)	**16**		
17	**Total deposits for quarter,** including overpayment applied from a prior quarter, from your records. ▶	**17**		
18	**Balance due** (subtract line 17 from line 16). This should be less than $500. Pay to IRS . . . ▶	**18**	109	44
19	Overpayment, if line 17 is more than line 16, enter here ▶ $ _____ and check if to be:			

☐ Applied to next return   **OR**   ☐ Refunded.

Record of Federal Tax Liability (You must complete if line 16 is $500 or more and Schedule B is not attached.) See instructions before checking these boxes

Check only if you made deposits using the 95% rule ▶ ☐   Check only if you are a first time 3-banking-day depositor. . . ▶ ☐

Date wages paid	Show tax liability here, **not deposits.** IRS gets deposit data from FTD coupons		
	First month of quarter	Second month of quarter	Third month of quarter
1st through 3rd	A	I	Q
4th through 7th	B	J	R
8th through 11th	C	K	S
12th through 15th	D	L	T
16th through 19th	E	M	U
20th through 22nd	F	N	V
23rd through 25th	G	O	W
26th through the last	H	P	X
Total liability for month	I	II	III

Do NOT Show Federal Tax Deposits Here

▶ **IV** Total for quarter (add lines **I, II,** and **III**). This should equal line 16 above . . . . . ▶

Sign Here
Under penalties of perjury, I declare that I have examined this return, including accompanying schedules and statements, and to the best of my knowledge and belief, it is true, correct, and complete.

Signature ▶   Print Your Name and Title ▶   Date ▶

FIGURE 35 Employer's Quarterly Tax Return

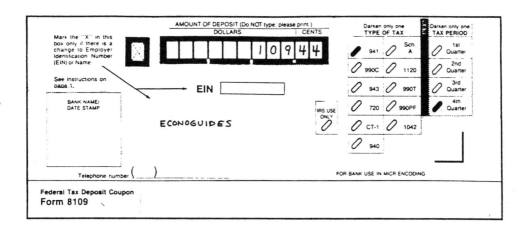

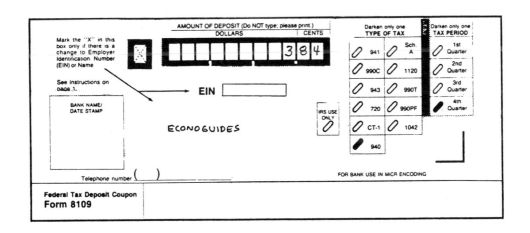

FIGURE 36 Federal Tax Deposit Coupon Form 8109

Form **940-EZ**		Employer's Annual Federal Unemployment (FUTA) Tax Return		OMB No. 1545-1110
Department of the Treasury Internal Revenue Service				1991

If incorrect, make any necessary changes. ▶	Name (as distinguished from trade name)
	Trade name, if any
	Address and ZIP code
	Employer identification number _

Follow the chart under "Who Can Use Form 940-EZ" on page 2. If you cannot use Form 940-EZ. you must use Form 940 instead.

A Enter the amount of contributions paid to your state unemployment fund. (See instructions for line A on page 4..▶ $ *14 44*

B (1) Enter the name of the state where you have to pay contributions . . . . ▶ ....

(2) Enter your state reporting number(s) as shown on state unemployment tax return. ▶ ....

If you will not have to file returns in the future, check here (see *Who Must File a Return* on page 2) **complete, and sign the return** . . ▶ ☐

If this is an Amended Return check here . . . . ▶ ☐

Part I   **Taxable Wages and FUTA Tax**

			Amount paid		
1	Total payments (including payments shown on lines 2 and 3) during the calendar year for services of employees	**1**			*480 00*
2	Exempt payments. (Explain all exempt payments, attaching additional sheets if necessary.) ▶	**2**			
3	Payments for services of more than $7,000. Enter only amounts over the first $7,000 paid to each employee. Do not include any exempt payments from line 2 . . .	**3**			
4	Total exempt payments (add lines 2 and 3)	**4**			
5	**Total taxable wages** (subtract line 4 from line 1) . . . . ▶	**5**			*480 00*
6	FUTA tax. Multiply the wages on line 5 by .008 and enter here. (If the result is over $100, also complete Part II.) .	**6**			*3 84*
7	Total FUTA tax deposited for the year. including any overpayment applied from a prior year (from your records)	**7**			
8	**Amount you owe** (subtract line 7 from line 6). This should be $100 or less. Pay to "Internal Revenue Service". ▶	**8**			*3 84*
9	Overpayment (subtract line 6 from line 7). Check if it is to be: ☐ **Applied to next return, or** ☐ Refunded ▶	**9**			

Part II   **Record of Quarterly Federal Unemployment Tax Liability** (Do not include state liability.) Complete only if line 6 is over $100.

Quarter	First (Jan. 1 – Mar. 31)	Second (Apr. 1 – June 30)	Third (July 1 – Sept. 30)	Fourth (Oct. 1 – Dec. 31)	Total for Year
Liability for quarter				*3.84*	*3.84*

Under penalties of perjury, I declare that I have examined this return, including accompanying schedules and statements, and, to the best of my knowledge and belief, it is true, correct, and complete, and that no part of any payment made to a state unemployment fund claimed as a credit was, or is to be, deducted from the payments to employees.

Signature ▶   Title (Owner, etc.) ▶   Date ▶

FIGURE 37   Federal Unemployment Return (FUTA)

102

1 Control number		OMB No. 1545-0008						

2 Employer's name, address, and ZIP code	6 Statutory employee ☐ Deceased ☐ Pension plan ☐ Legal rep. ☐ 942 emp. ☐ Subtotal ☐ Deferred compensation ☐ Void ☐

ECONOGUIDES

	7 Allocated tips	8 Advance EIC payment
	9 Federal income tax withheld **36.00**	10 Wages, tips, other compensation **480.00**

3 Employer's identification number	4 Employer's state I.D. number	11 Social security tax withheld **29.76**	12 Social security wages **480.00**
5 Employee's social security number		13 Social security tips	14 Medicare wages and tips **480.00**

19 Employee's name, address, and ZIP code	15 Medicare tax withheld **6.96**	16 Nonqualified plans
ALEXANDRA	17 See Instrs. for Box 17	18 Other

20 /////	21 /////	22 Dependent care benefits	23 Benefits included in Box 10

24 State income tax **6.28**	25 State wages, tips, etc. **480.00**	26 Name of state	27 Local income tax	28 Local wages, tips, etc.	29 Name of locality

Copy B To Be Filed With Employee's FEDERAL Tax Return   Department of the Treasury—Internal Revenue Service

Form **W-2** **Wage and Tax Statement 1991**

1 Control number		OMB No. 1545-0008		

Kind of Payer ▶	2 941/941E ☑ Military ☐ 943 ☐ CT-1 ☐ 942 ☐ Medicare govt. emp. ☐	3 Employer's state I.D. number 4	5 Total number of statements **1**

6 Establishment number	7 Allocated tips	8 Advance EIC payments
9 Federal income tax withheld **36.00**	10 Wages, tips, and other compensation **480.00**	11 Social security tax withheld **29.76**
12 Social security wages **480.00**	13 Social security tips	14 Medicare wages and tips **480.00**
15 Medicare tax withheld **6.96**	16 Nonqualified plans	17 Deferred compensation
18 Employer's identification number		19 Other EIN used this year
20 Employer's name		21 Dependent care benefits
		23 Adjusted total social security wages and tips
		24 Adjusted total Medicare wages and tips
		25 Income tax withheld by third-party payer
22 Employer's address and ZIP code		

Form **W-3** **Transmittal of Income and Tax Statements 1991**   Department of the Treasury Internal Revenue Service

FIGURE 38   W-2 Statement & W-3 Transmittal

□ VOID	□ CORRECTED

PAYER'S name, street address, city, state, and ZIP code	1 Rents $	OMB No. 1545-0115	Miscellaneous Income
ECONOGUIDES	2 Royalties $	19**91**	
	3 Prizes, awards, etc. $		

PAYER'S Federal identification number	RECIPIENT'S identification number	4 Federal income tax withheld $	5 Fishing boat proceeds $	
RECIPIENT'S name		6 Medical and health care payments $	7 Nonemployee compensation $ *690.00*	
TEMP SERVICES INC.		8 Substitute payments in lieu of dividends or interest $	9 Payer made direct sales of $5,000 or more of consumer products to a buyer (recipient) for resale ▶ □	Copy 1 For State Tax Department
Street address (including apt. no.)				
City, state, and ZIP code		10 Crop insurance proceeds $	11 State income tax withheld $	
Account number (optional)		12 State/Payer's state number		

Form **1099-MISC**   Department of the Treasury - Internal Revenue Service

---

DO NOT STAPLE   6969   □ CORRECTED

Form **1096** Department of the Treasury Internal Revenue Service	**Annual Summary and Transmittal of U.S. Information Returns**	OMB No 1545-0108 19**91**

ATTACH IRS LABEL HERE

Type or machine print FILER'S name (or attach label)
ECONOGUIDES
Street address (room or suite number)

City, state, and ZIP code

	Name of person to contact if IRS needs more information	**For Official Use Only**
If you are not using a preprinted label, enter in Box 1 or 2 below the identification number you used as the filer on the information returns being transmitted. Do not fill in both Boxes 1 and 2.	Telephone number ( )	□□□□□□□ □□

1 Employer identification number	2 Social security number	3 Total number of documents /	4 Federal income tax withheld $	5 Total amount reported with this Form 1096 $ *690.00*

Check only one box below to indicate the type of form being transmitted. | If this is your FINAL return, check here . . . ▶ □

W-2G 32	1098 81	1099-A 80	1099-B 79	1099-DIV 91	1099-G 86	1099-INT 92	1099-MISC 95 ✓	1099-OID 96	1099-PATR 97	1099-R 98	1099-S 75	5498 28

Under penalties of perjury, I declare that I have examined this return and accompanying documents, and, to the best of my knowledge and belief, they are true, correct, and complete.

Signature ▶ .... Title ▶ .... Date ▶ ....

FIGURE 39 Form 1099 MISC & 1096 Transmittal

Balance Sheet Analysis

The following formulas are used by creditors and investors to determine financial strength and weakness of a company (the numbers used in the examples are those from the balance sheet and P&L statements of 12-31-91).

Working Capital

Measures a company's ability to overcome a temporary financial crisis.

Current Assets - Current Liabilities   4690 - 3040 = 1650

The working capital figure may be compared with the average monthly cash expenses to indicate how long the business could operate if it experienced a slow down in sales or collections. Since the total cash expenses for the year were about $15,800, the working capital of $1650 would cover operations for a little over a month.

Current Ratio

Measures whether the business has enough current assets to meet its current debts with a margin of safety. The ratio is

$$\frac{\textbf{Current Assets}}{\textbf{Current Liabilities}} \qquad \frac{4690}{3040} = 1.5$$

This shows there are 1.5 dollars of assets for every dollar of debt. As a general rule, $2 of assets for every $1 debt is considered a good current ratio. Manufacturing businesses often need ratios of 3 to 1, whereas restaurants with less inventory value can be in good financial shape with ratios less than 2 to 1.

Acid-Test Ratio

Is a more exacting measure of ability to pay a current debt.

$$\frac{\textbf{Cash + Receivables}}{\textbf{Current Liabilities}} \qquad \frac{4030}{3040} = 1.3$$

There is 1.3 dollars available for every dollar of current debt. A 1 to 1 ratio is usually considered satisfactory if all the accounts receivable are collectible.

One might think that high Current and Acid-Test ratios is good. However, high ratios can also signal idle cash, delinquent accounts and high inventories all of which would be costing the business money. The owner's job is to make sure all the resources are working as hard as possible. Two measures that help do that are the Average Collection Period and Inventory Turnover.

Average Collection Period

The average number of days it takes to collect from credit sales which indicates the quality of credit accounts and effectiveness of collection methods. This figure involves a two-step calculation using the total credit sales figure from the P&L Statement to calculate the amount of credit sales per day. This figure is then divided into the Accounts Receivable from the Balance Sheet to determine the average collection period.

Step 1:

Total Credit Sales	$7200	= $20 credit sales
365 Days	365	per day

Step 2:

Accounts Receivable	$600	= 30 day average
Credit Sales Per Day	$20	collection

An average collection period of 30 days is acceptable. The general rule is that the average shouldn't exceed the company's payment terms by more than 1/3. If payment terms are the customary net 30, the Average Collection Period should be less than 40 days (1/3 of 30 = 10; 30 + 10 = 40). The Average Collection Period should be calculated periodically and collection procedures or terms changed if necessary. Recent trends have been to shorter terms of net 10 and net 20.

Inventory Turnover

Shows how fast products are moving.

Cost of Goods Sold	3260	= 10 times
Average Inventory	320	per year

The Cost of Goods Sold figure is taken from P&L Statement. The average inventory figure is the beginning inventory (or initial stocking) plus the ending inventory divided by 2 (300 + 340 ÷ 2 = 320). Generally, the higher the turnover the better,— provided small reorders are economical and won't result in shortages. High turnover suggests inventories are current and salable; low inventory turnover indicates slow sales and unsalable merchandise.

Return
on Investment

Perhaps the best measure of profitability.

$$\frac{\textbf{Net Profit}}{\textbf{Total Assets}} \times 100 \qquad \frac{1005}{6290} \times 100 = 16\%$$

This measure of profit is considered better than that computed from P&L Statements because it shows profit as a percentage of <u>all</u> of the assets being used. The Return on Investment figure is one lenders and investors look at very closely to see how it compares with other returns available to them. For example, a well managed florist or bakery has 25% to 30% return on investment (lenders would also know the indicated 16% return is illusionary as the owner was not paid for his time).

Equity-to-Debt

This measure is taken from the right hand (liabilities) side of the Balance Sheet and has become an important indicator of financial strength. The ratio is computed by determining the percent of the total liability that is represented by equity, and subtracting that from 100 to find the percentage which is represented by debt.

$$\frac{\textbf{Equity}}{\textbf{Total Liabilities}} \times 100 \qquad \frac{970}{6290} \times 100 = 15\%$$

If the Equity is 15%, the remaining 85% is debt. Therefore, the *Equity-to-Debt ratio is 15% to 85%.* This would be considered a very weak ratio. The Equity to Debt ratio of leading corporations is commonly in the 75% to 25% range. The good news is that this company doesn't have to worry about a hostile takeover!

Sources of published business ratios include:

- *Almanac of Business and Industrial Financial Ratios*, by Leo Troy, Prentice Hall.

- *Annual Statement Studies,* published annually by Robert Morris Associates. Covers 300 lines of business. Philadelphia National Bank Building, Philadelphia, PA 19107.

- *Key Business Ratios,* published annually by Dun and Bradstreet, Inc., 99 Church St., New York, NY 10007. Covers 125 lines of business activity, including manufacturing, wholesaling, retailing, and construction industries.

- *Special Reports*, published from time to time by trade and professional associations, major accounting firms, financial magazines, and universities.

Loan Record

Preparing balance sheets is made easier by keeping a record of loan balances similar to that shown in Figure 40. The loan date, amount and terms are noted when the loan is made and updated annually showing the principal repaid and loan balance (supplied by lender). A column showing the amounts due within the next 12 months is helpful for determining "current liabilities."

CREDITOR	DATE	AMOUNT	TERMS	REPAID PRINCIPAL	TIME BALANCE	DUE NEXT 12 MOS
UNION BANK	1-10-91	500	12%/YR	500	0	0
CREDIT UNION	6-10-91	3,600	36@120	600	3,720	1,440
MT. MICRO	12-1-91	800	4@200	0	800	800
TOTAL	1991	4,900		1,100	4,520	2,240
	1992					
CREDIT UNION		3,720				
MT. MICRO		800				

FIGURE 40 Loan Record

109

Inventory Management

Finding Inventory Value Without A Physical Count

Given:

Beginning Inventory 1-1-92	$ 340
Goods Purchased 1st Qtr 92	4200
Cost of Goods	4
Sale Price of Goods	11
Sales Income 1st Qtr 92	7700

Find: Inventory value at end of 1st quarter.

Solution: $1,768

1. Find ratio of cost of goods to sales price (4 ÷ 11) = .36
2. Find cost of goods sold by multiplying income by cost to sales ratio (7,700 X .36) = $2,772.
3. Find ending inventory value by subtracting cost of goods sold from total inventory available during period (340 + 4,200 - 2,772) = $1,768.

Note that "given" data is always available so inventory levels can always be obtained using this method.

Finding Annual Inventory Turnover

Given:

Beginning 1st Qtr. Inventory	$ 340
Ending 1st Qtr. Inventory	1768
Cost of Goods Sold	2772

Find: Annual inventory turnover.

Solution: 10.4

$$\text{Turnover} = \frac{\text{Cost of Goods Sold}}{\text{Average Inventory}}$$

$$= \frac{2772}{(340 + 1,768) \div 2}$$

$$= \frac{2772}{1054}$$

$$= 2.6 \text{ (1st quarter) OR}$$
$$10.4 \text{ Annually}$$

Note that the annual turnover is simply the quarterly rate multiplied by 4. The annual turnover rate may be computed and compared at the end of each quarter for any signs of weakness (decrease in turnover). The calculation can cover any period of time; if period selected is 2 months, the resulting rate would be multiplied by 6 to get the annual rate.

Finding Minimum Order Quantities

Given:

Annual Use	= 3,250 books and mailing envelopes
Unit Cost	
Printing $2.70	
Envelope $ .30	
Postage $1.00	= $ 4.00
Ordering Cost	= $15.00 (national average)
Carrying Cost	= 25% (national average)

Find: Minimum order quantities for books and mailing envelope:

Solution: 1100

$$\sqrt{\frac{2 \text{ X Typical Annual Use in Units X Order Cost}}{\text{Unit Cost X Carrying Cost \% per Year}}} = \text{Minimum Order}$$

Minimum Book Order:

$$= \sqrt{\frac{2 \text{ X } 3250 \text{ X } 15}{2.70 \text{ X } .25}}$$

$$= \sqrt{\frac{97,500}{.68}}$$

$$= \sqrt{143,382}$$

$$= 379 *$$

* The better calculators have a square root key; simply enter number and touch key to find answer.

Minimum Envelope Order:

$$= \sqrt{\frac{2 \times 3250 \times 15}{.30 \times .25}}$$

$$= \sqrt{\frac{97,500}{.08}}$$

$$= \sqrt{1,218,750}$$

$$= 1,104$$

Important!

Formula answers are only guides which must be adjusted to real world pricing. For example, 379 is not a realistic number for printing books. The cost of setting up a press is such that printing 1000 copies costs little more than printing 400. Since 3,250 books will be needed, 3 orders of 1100 each will be placed, which will allow for some imperfect books which can be returned for credit later. The order will be matched with 3 orders of 1100 envelopes (recommended minimum).

The formula will always result in smaller, more frequent orders of high cost goods, and larger, less frequent orders of low cost goods. This is the essence of good inventory management: *minimize money* tied up in costly items and *minimize the time* spent on low-cost items, which is what the formulas will help you achieve. You'll probably find that 20% of the inventory items will represent 80% of the inventory value, and this is where most of the time and attention should be focused.

Finding Lead Time Needed For Orders

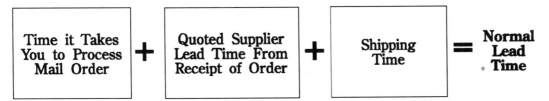

Solution: Envelopes

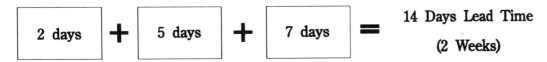

Finding Safety Supply Needed

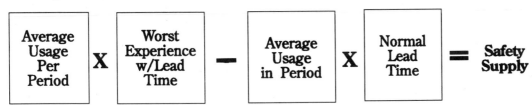

Solution: Envelopes

| 63 | **X** | 5 | **—** | 63 | **X** | 2 | **=** | 189 Safety Supply |

* Average weekly use = 3,250 ÷ 52 = 63

Finding The Reorder Point

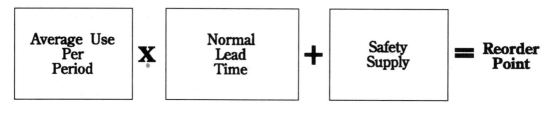

Solution: Envelopes

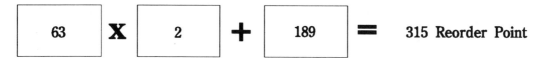

Envelopes will need to be
reordered when supply reaches 300 and a
REORDER! marker is placed at
that point in the supply.

System Options For The Growing Business

One-Write Systems

When you're sending out more than 30 checks a month a fair amount of time is spent writing. Consider what's involved in paying one bill: you write the check; you write key information on the check stub; and you address the envelope for mailing. *One-write* systems combine these three separate steps into one by using carbon-backed checks and double-window envelopes. As you write the check, the carbon transfers the date, payee's name, check number, and amount onto a record sheet. A special binder holds the check in place and keeps the carbon entries aligned. By entering the street address in the space provided under the payee's name, the check may be put into a double-window envelope and mailed.

The one-write system eliminates the need for sorting checks into expense categories at the end of the month. Instead, the dollar amount of each check, shown on the record sheet, can be entered under the proper expense category *on the same sheet*. The record sheet is then totaled and cross checked in the same way as explained for the Financial Summary.

Figure 41 shows how the January expenses would appear on a one-write system. Note how the check amounts are also recorded under the appropriate category at right (for illustration purposes only the first four expense categories are shown). Note also that an expense may be divided among several categories. For example, the check to reimburse owner for expenses is divided among telephone, supplies and other appropriate categories. The record sheet may be cross-checked for accuracy: the sum of all the checks written during the month ($1,153.00) should equal to the sum of all the category totals added across. The record sheet also provides a place to enter bank deposits and bank balance. The end of month bank balance is simply the sum of all the deposits including interest ($1,472.50) less the sum of all checks written and any bank charges ($1,153.00) or $319.50. The back of the record sheet provides space for summarizing the *income* by category, as well as the end-of-month bank balance computation so all financial data for the period are on one sheet.

117

DISBURSEMENTS JOURNAL

MONTH __JANUARY 1991__

#	DATE	TO THE ORDER OF	DESCRIPTION	CHECK NUMBER	√	CHECK AMOUNT	DEPOSITS DATE	DEPOSITS AMOUNT	BANK BALANCE	MERCH	ADVERT	TELE	SUPP
									0.00				
1	1-2	LOCAL COUNTY	BUSINESS NAME	101	√	6 00	1-5	1000 00					
2	1-2	STATE DEPT OF REVENUE	RETAIL SALE LICENSE	102	√	5 00							
3	1-5	OFFICE SERVICE & SUPPLY	FURNITURE-OFFICE	103	√	235 00							
4	1-9	TABLEROCK PRINTERS	ADVERTISING	104	√	165 10					165 10		
5	1-15	POSTMASTER	AD POSTAGE	105	√	150 00					150 00		
6	1-15	BRUCE VARIETY	SUPPLIES	106	√	36 15							36 15
7	1-15	PROFESSIONAL OFFICE SUPPLY	SUPPLIES	107	√	122 35	1-18	52 50					122 35
8	1-23	TABLEROCK PRINTERS	BOOKS	108		200 00				200 00			
9	1-24	POSTMASTER	BOOK POSTAGE	109	√	100 00	1-25	73 00 / 250 00		100 00			
10	1-31	DEPT OF REVENUE	SALES TAX	110		10 50							
11	1-31	OWNER	REIMBURSE EXPENSES	111		122 90	1-28	94 50				40 75	2 00
12		BANK CHGS				0 00		Int 2 00					
13		TOTAL JANUARY				1153 00		1,472 50	319 50	300 00	315 10	40 75	160 50
14													
15													

EconoGuides

7473/2531

112

PAY					CHECK AMOUNT
DATE	TO THE ORDER OF		DESCRIPTION	CHECK NO.	$

DOLLARS

Union Bank

⑈253 7473 ⑈: 0⑈7758⑈ 112

FIGURE 41 One-write System Record Sheet

**Bookkeeping
Services**

Somewhere between the time you've mastered financial record-keeping and the business reaches a level where you have no time for them, you should be considering a part-time bookkeeper or bookkeeping service. How quickly that time comes depends on the complexity as well as the volume of the business. For example, businesses involving employees, inventories, and credit sales will reach that point faster than those whose operations don't involve such complexities.

Contracting for bookkeeping services instead of hiring a bookkeeper can be cost effective because you save payroll taxes and insurance expenses. But the advantages of contracting must be weighed against the additional cost of such services and loss of some control and privacy. One approach is to determine the price and quality of a contract service and compare that to the cost, availability, record keeping and liability involved in hiring a qualified part-time employee.

Automated Systems

You can buy micro-computer software that makes the proper bookkeeping entries automatically, so there is no need for a trained bookkeeper or service. You, or an employee, simply enter the dollar amount and category of any income or expense item and the software does the rest. What many forget is that these automated systems still require that *someone* sit down and enter the correct dollar figure and category. The only real difference between data entry in automated and manual systems is that one is entered with the stroke of a key, and the other a stroke of a pencil. The accuracy of each method depends entirely on how carefully the entry is made. The real payoff of an automated system is in the quantity and quality of the *output* it produces. For instance, you can buy software that will print out checks, invoices, accounts receivable and payable, inventory balances, payroll tax reports and financial statements. Such software costs hundreds of dollars but can quickly pay for itself in time saved.

When estimating or comparing automation costs, include the costs of computer equipment, computer paper and forms, printer ribbons, equipment maintenance, and the time needed to master the hardware and software. You should consider automating when you can no longer keep up with *output* needs manually. No question that printed reports and graphics look more professional, but ask yourself if they are really needed to run and grow the business. If not, you could save a lot of time and money.

The time spent developing a manual system is never wasted. If you're having a hard time making it work by hand, a machine will probably not help you much. When you do automate, consider keeping the same or similar income and expense categories so you can compare figures with those of prior years.

Petty Cash Fund

As the business grows, it may become more convenient to have cash on hand to pay for such unexpected expenses as courier or package delivery services charges or small office supplies. This is done by creating a petty cash fund. The fund is established by writing and cashing a check to Petty Cash ($20 to $200, depending on need) and placing cash in a locked box accessible to the person who will be responsible for the fund. The petty cash is then exchanged for receipts which are kept in the lock box. When cash gets low, it is restored to the original amount by issuing a check equal to and in exchange for the receipts in the box. Petty cash receipts are stapled and totalled by category and included with other category expenses to determine Earnings Record totals in the normal manner. If any cash overage develops in the fund, it is deposited as "other" income; any shortage is noted and included as "miscellaneous" expense. The Petty Cash Fund is included as a Cash Asset on the balance sheet.

Purchase Order System

As suppliers and supply orders increase, you'll want to add a purchase order system. The system uses Purchase Order forms and a clipboard in the same way as invoice forms and Accounts Receivable clipboard are used. The procedure is as follows: a copy of the purchase order sent to the supplier is kept on the clipboard until the order comes in. At that time, the purchase order is removed, compared with the goods and supplier's bill received, then placed with the bill in the expense envelope. Purchase orders on the clipboard represent "payables" and are handy for figuring cash flow or the balance sheet. You may want to consider pre-numbered, imprinted, two-copy forms if you have a lot of suppliers and inventory orders. Otherwise, you can get by with photocopying the form provided as needed. In any case, only *one person* should be authorized to issue purchase orders.

Business Investment Account

While banks provide a great deal of convenience and service, spare funds can usually earn more interest in a money market or other mutual fund account. Professional managers consider money market mutual funds as safe as federally insured bank deposits. Most money market mutual funds offer unlimited check writing of amounts over $500. In addition to having your balance earning more interest, you often benefit from the additional time it can take for a check to clear such an account. Money market mutual funds are administered by investment firms and shouldn't be confused with the "money market investment accounts" offered by banks which are insured accounts usually offering lower interest.

It's important to note that even after establishing an investment account, *all income continues to be deposited in the business bank account and all expenses continue to be paid from checks drawn on this bank account.* Spare funds are transferred to the investment account with a business bank account check, and the amount recorded as a "non-deductible expense" on the Financial Summary. If investment funds are needed for operations, an investment account check (usually $500 or more) is written payable to the business and deposited in the business bank account; the amount is recorded as "non-taxable" income on Financial Summary. At the end of the year, you will be notified of the amount of interest the investment account earned, and this amount is entered on the December Financial Summary as "interest" income.

Asset Management Account

When your business has sufficient funds, you should consider an Asset Management Account offered by major brokerages, Mutual Funds and large financial institutions. Such accounts can serve as combination bank and investment accounts as they provide:

- unlimited check writing
- money market rates on any surplus funds
- major credit card with high limit
- low cost brokerage services
- one consolidated monthly statement

The drawbacks are:

- minimums needed to open accounts
- having to mail or bank-wire deposits
- concentration of financial assets
- loss of control over confidential information
- accounts not insured by the U.S. government
- annual fees (currently under $100)

Note that by charging all business travel on the account's credit card and noting a two-digit, expense category code on each check, you could have a very low cost automated financial record system. The reason is the detailed monthly statements provide subtotals for each expense category as well as beginning and ending account balance.

7 Helpful Hints For Selling The Business

1. **Determine the fair market value.**
   If the majority of assets are intangible, such as trademarks, copyrights, patents, or secret processes, you should seek assistance from attorneys and other specialists in intellectual property. Also seek expert advise if you have large and specialized customer lists, inventory and equipment. Otherwise, you can get a fair estimate using the Business Valuation form.

2. **Prepare a business plan and budget for next 3 years.**
   Show projected earnings, how sales targets will be met by marketing existing or new products and how you plan to maintain competitive advantage, quality and cost control.

3. **Make sure books reflect true earnings.**
   Reduce non-essential expenses and benefits; owner's pay should be competitive with what a manager would earn for an equivalent amount of time. That also applies to spouse and other family members working in the business.

4. **List and feel out potential buyers.**
   The list might include your competitors, associates, suppliers and employees. Determine interest, possibly through a third party, being careful not to start rumors than might harm the business.

5. **Consider using a business broker.**
   A broker can help you locate a buyer and negotiate the deal. Ask trusted friends and associates for referrals, or consult a trade or professional organization. Speak to several of the broker's recent clients.

6. **Be patient.**
   Most sales take a year or more to complete. Use the time to continue to build the business and make it even more attractive to buyers. Think through the terms you'd accept: lowest price; how long you can wait for full payment; and what role, time, commitment, and pay you would accept to stay on with the business after the sale.

7. **Have an experienced attorney and tax adviser review the sales agreement before you sign.**
   Your attorney can ensure that any non-compete agreement is reasonable, and that your interests, including payments promised, are protected. Your tax advisor can suggest strategies such as installment sales, exchanging stock or other like-kind exchanges to reduce or defer taxes on the sale.

Personal Income and Expense Categories

Income Categories

Earnings

Gross wages, salaries, commissions, bonuses, tips, fees, and taxable benefits received for services reported on W-2 and 1099 MISC forms.

Interest

Sums earned on deposits at financial institutions and on taxable bonds. Dividends paid on money market mutual funds are considered interest and should be included here.

Dividends

Sums earned on individual stocks and stock mutual funds.

Business

Includes earnings from proprietorships, partnerships, rental real estate, and other business's investments. Annual earnings are usually reported on K-1 and 1099 forms.

Payments

Taxable payments received such as unemployment, alimony, and employer paid disability.

Social Security

Payments from the Social Security administration are reported on Federal Form SSA 1099. Up to one half the amount is taxable if adjusted gross income exceeds stated limits ($25,000 for single person or $32,000 married couple filing jointly in 1991).

Capital Gains

Gains from sale of securities, real estate, collectibles or other investments. Currently taxed as ordinary income at rates from 15% to 33% depending on taxable income level.

Non-taxable

Non-taxable income such as loans, gifts, bequests, proceeds from life and casualty insurance claims, reimbursements for business expenses, or tax refunds.

Expense Categories

Taxes

Amounts withheld or paid for Federal, state, and local income and Social Security taxes. These sums are reported on Federal W-2 forms, estimated tax payments, and comparable state forms.

Housing

Payments on home mortgage and improvement loans or rent; amounts paid for furnishings and appliances, maintenance and repair; amounts paid for property taxes (homeowner insurance is usually included under Insurance as it also covers personal property and liability).

Utilities & Telephone	Payments for light, heat, air conditioning, water and sewer, garbage removal; monthly residential phone service and personal long distance calls (business calls are shown on Schedule C).
Insurance	Premiums paid for life, disability, liability, and homeowner policies (auto insurance is included with transportation; single premium life and annuity policy payments are included under Savings).
Food	Groceries, household supplies, meals out.
Clothing and Personal Care	Includes purchase, alterations, cleaning and repair of clothing and amounts spent for personal grooming and appearance including hair, skin and nail care, massage, and fitness.
Medical	Includes medical insurance premiums, out-of-pocket costs of doctor, dentists, prescriptions, and medications, and transportation expenses including use of personal auto (currently 9 cents per mile or actual direct operating costs). Sums that exceed 7.5% of adjusted gross income are deductible as itemized expenses.
Transportation	Car loan payments, fuel, maintenance and repair, license and auto insurance premiums, parking, tolls and other commuting expenses (auto expenses while on vacation travel should be included under Recreation).
Recreation	Amounts spent for entertainment and hobbies, club memberships, and vacation travel, hotels, meals, and admission fees.
Education	Amounts spent on educating children and adult family members; includes tuition, books, supplies. Business and professional memberships, subscriptions, and courses required to maintain job skills are deductible business expense on Schedule C, or if working for someone else, as a miscellaneous expense on Schedule A on amounts exceeding 2% of adjusted gross income.
Contributions	Donations to educational, religious, charitable, and social institutions. Donations must be tax deductible before they can be included as itemized deductions. They can include the fair market value of donated goods. Rule of thumb for market value is 15% of purchase price. The use of personal car for charitable work is also deductible, currently at 9 cents per mile.

Gifts and Miscellaneous	Sums spent on birthday, anniversary, wedding, and other celebrations. This category is also used for various miscellaneous expenses. Safety deposit box rental and management fees on IRA accounts are miscellaneous expenses which are deductible when all such income-related miscellaneous expenses exceed the 2% of adjusted gross income.
Professional Fees	Amounts paid to attorneys, accountants, and other advisors. Tax preparation and certain legal and professional fees are tax deductible as miscellaneous, subject to the 2% minimum.
Support Payments	Amounts paid for alimony and child support. Alimony payments and related legal expenses are deductible; child support payments are not.
Child Care	Amounts spent for child care in the home or at child care centers. This is a major expense, averaging about 8% of income in families where both parents work. Federal and state governments provide significant tax credits to help offset child care expenses of working parents.
Loans	Amounts spent on repayments of *personal loans*. (Installment payments on goods should be shown under category of purchase such as car payments under Transportation and furniture under Housing). Interest on personal loans is not deductible, unless the loan is secured by the equity in a home.
Savings	Contributions to IRA, savings accounts, mutual funds, annuities, or single premium life insurance. IRA contributions are currently fully deductible if not covered by an employer retirement plan or if adjusted gross income is under $25,000 for single taxpayers and $40,000 for couple filing jointly. Limited deductions apply if the adjusted gross income is between $25,000 and $35,000 for a single person, and between $40,000 and $50,000 for couples filing jointly. Interest and dividends earned on IRA accounts, annuities and insurance products are tax deferred until withdrawn; interest on "public purpose" bonds issued by states and municipalities is tax exempt.

Helpful Hints on Personal Records Management

**Financial
Records
Envelope**

Place monthly bank and credit card statements, canceled checks, credit card slips, electric, telephone, and other household bills in a 9" X 12" envelope. Replace bank credit card, telephone and other bulky statements in envelopes they came in before putting them into the 9"x12" manila envelope. This will allow you to fit more into your envelope and simplifies sorting at the end of the year. One or two such envelopes should be sufficient for a year's financial records. There's no need to summarize monthly household expenditures as you do for the business. At year's end sort checks, bills and credit card slips into major categories to track where money is going and project expenses and savings for the coming year.

If you plan to itemize deductions on your tax return, keep the canceled checks supporting those deductions as well as canceled checks for major household or personal property purchases for proof of gains or losses. (By making your larger charitable contributions in December, it'll be easier to stay within your budget and earn interest in the meantime). With those exceptions, it is safe to discard household bills and canceled checks when you've completed your annual summary. Some persons prefer to hold on to all records for one year.

File tax returns and documentation in 9" X 12" manila envelopes by year. Technically, you're required to keep tax data for 3 years after the due date of the return (April 15, 1995 for 1991 return). However, if you substantially under-reported your income, the IRS has an additional 2 years in which to challenge. And, if the IRS feels the under-reporting was intentional (can you say fraud?) there is *no time limit* for challenge. So it's best to keep returns about 5 or 6 years . If your returns are simple and you take the standard deduction, there's no reason to hold on to canceled checks and receipts except where you might feel better with proof of payment.

Securities

Original certificates or other proof of purchase for stocks, bonds, and other securities should be kept in separate folders together with notices of annual dividends and stock splits so that future gains or losses can be reported accurately and substantiated if the return is audited.

Retirement Accounts

Make separate folders for IRA, KEOGH and company pension plans and file all papers and balance statements relating to these plans in the folders. For tax purposes, all such records should be kept indefinitely.

Insurance Policies

Make separate folders for Auto, Life, Disability and Property insurance. Note the specific policies contained in each folder on the inside front cover. Don't forget group policies provided by your employer or membership organizations. Discard the old policies when you insert the new ones. Keep canceled checks on any private disability policies to prove benefits are not taxable.

Home(s)

Keep all financial records relating to the purchase of your home(s) and any improvements made. Such records will establish gains or losses for tax purposes.

Household Inventory

A detailed inventory of household furnishings and possessions is required by insurance companies before settling loss claims. It's a lot easier to do this before rather than after the loss. A quick inventory can be made by taking photos (or a video) of each room and contents. Detailed description, including purchase price, can be written on the back of photos of more valuable items. This inventory must be updated and kept outside the residence (see Safe Deposit Box).

Warranties

File all current warranties on auto, boat, and home in file marked warranties. Add new warranties in front, and occasionally check and discard outdated warranties in the back of the folder. Operating and maintenance instructions should be kept separately—usually with or near the equipment or appliance.

Health Records	Keep records of immunizations and illnesses, allergies, and medications for all family members. Such records are helpful in diagnosis and treatment as well as prevention of illness and genetic counseling.
Education & Employment	Educational transcripts, military and employment records including duties, responsibilities, and performance appraisals are useful in claiming benefits and preparing resumes and employment history.
Wills	Copies of wills, letters of instruction, and contents of safe deposit box should be kept in a safe place at home. The originals should be filed with your attorney or executor.
Net Worth Statements	Copies of periodic financial statements, including those filed for loan applications, are helpful in tracking financial progress and long term planning.
Safe Deposit Box	Keep hard to replace papers in a bank safe deposit box. For example:

- birth certificates, adoption papers
- designation of social security number
- military discharge papers
- passports, citizenship papers
- marriage and death certificates, divorce decrees
- powers of attorney
- titles and deeds (auto and property)
- partnership agreements, important contracts
- bonds and certificates of deposits
- copyrights, trademarks, and patents
- household inventory and photos
- promissory notes and records of moneys owed you
- insurance policies (optional).

Do *not* keep in safe deposit box:
- cash (not insured, earns no interest, suspicious)
- rare coins and jewelry (not insured)
- original of will (box may be sealed upon death)

Helpful Hints To Increase Savings

Pay Yourself First

The most effective savings strategy is "pay yourself first". The best way to implement this strategy is as follows: first, determine the percentage of income you've decided to save and indicate the dollar amount as Savings on a budget worksheet. Next, fill in all the fixed expenses such as housing, loans, insurance premiums, utilities, and so on. Finally, estimate the variable expenses such as food, clothing, recreation until 100% of income is accounted for.

If you have been saving 5% of your income and would like to save 10%, the additional 5% will have to come from cutting down on the variable expenses. Divide all figures by 12 to estimate the monthly expenses. If you don't think you can manage on the amounts allocated, aim for saving 7% as it's more important to set a goal you can achieve. Then, "pay yourself first" by making the savings deposit *before* you pay any other monthly bills. Fight any temptation to skip a month by having the deposit drawn from your checking account or payroll check automatically. This is an especially good idea when the employer is matching a portion of your savings in a tax deferred 401(k) or 403(b) plan. Many employers will make automatic deductions for purchases of U.S. Savings Bonds which have some important tax advantages. Banks will make automatic monthly transfers from checking account to higher paying savings accounts. Or, you can authorize your mutual fund to automatically debit your personal bank account each month. Whatever the means, the sooner you begin a regular savings program, the sooner you will be earning rather than paying interest.

Buy Low

You can increase your savings by using smart shopping techniques. The objective is to buy quality products at competitive prices. Quality doesn't mean top of the line; usually the whistles and bells, not to mention hype, aren't worth the price. On the other hand, the stripped-down versions may not fully satisfy. The best values are often found in mid-range price levels. Contact discount retailers and suppliers to establish the best price, but don't overlook the convenience and advantage offered by local dealers. If the product requires regular service it's usually worth the additional cost to buy locally.

133

Buy Low ...

New Cars & Appliances: Check local library or book stands for new car price guides so you know what the model costs the dealer. Add-on options such as maintenance contracts, dealer financing, and life insurance are usually not worth the cost. For instance, home appliances and computers can be expected to give long, trouble-free service and you'll do better by paying for repairs as needed. Similarly, the cost of life insurance and dealer financing provided as part of the contract is often very high. If you're required to accept any of these options as part of the deal, try elsewhere.

Used Cars & Second Hand Goods: Since most depreciation occurs in the first year or two, you can buy a like-new big ticket item for close to half its original cost. You can assure that it *is* nearly as good as new by paying a professional to inspect it. Many dealers guarantee used equipment; if not, then a reasonably priced maintenance agreement might be a good bet. Before buying a car or major appliance, look up its record in consumer magazines at your local library. There are many bargains in used furniture, clothing, recreational equipment, toys, and books. Check newspapers, second hand stores, and yard sales before heading to the mall.

Homes: As the biggest single purchase most families ever make, the price paid for a home has major and lasting impact on personal finances. The following guidelines will help assure a good purchase price:

- look for bargain prices under foreclosures, pre-foreclosures, and estate sales in local papers, at banks, lending agencies and court houses. You can also contact: Department of Housing and Urban Development (HUD), and Resolution Trust Corporation (RTC) and Department of Veterans' Affairs (DVA) in Washington, DC about foreclosed properties near you.

- look for run down or lower priced houses in better neighborhoods.

- don't be afraid to offer much less than the asking price (10% or more is common). Closing costs are negotiable, sellers have been known to pay all.

- make any offer and deposit contingent on: a satisfactory report by professional inspector or engineer; securing a mortgage loan you can afford; and selling your existing home (if necessary).

- keep in mind that real estate agents work for the *sellers* and will have their interests in mind. You can hire an agent to act as *your* broker in finding and inspecting the property, negotiating the price, suggesting mortgage lenders, structuring the offer and expediting the sale. If real estate transactions and hard negotiating are not your thing, it could be money very well spent.

- shop for a favorable mortgage as carefully as you do the home. Since most mortgages are resold, concentrate on the terms rather than the lender.

- find an attorney who specializes in real estate and works for a flat fee to represent you at the closing. Don't try to close a real estate transaction without legal representation; you be risking your financial future in order to save a few hundred dollars. It simply isn't worth it.

Defer Taxes

Whenever possible, savings should be placed in tax deferred accounts especially if you are in the 28% federal bracket or higher. By deferring taxes you savings grow much faster because of compound interest, and you'll ultimately pay less tax because you will likely be subject to a lower tax rate when you retire. That strategy has worked until now and, while not guaranteed, is not unreasonable to expect in the future. Taxed deferred accounts include:

- IRA
- KEOGH or SEP
- Company Savings Plans 401(k) or 403(b)
- Company Pension Plans

When available savings exceed the maximum annual contributions allowed in the above accounts, the following tax-advantaged investments should be considered:

135

Defer Taxes . . .

Paying Down Mortgage - Using savings to pay down mortgage principal can be a good strategy when mortgage interest is 2% or more than you could earn on other investments. Gains from sale of residences are tax deferred and tax free up to $125,000 on sales made after 55 years of age.

Municipal Bond and Bond Funds - Most municipalities issue bonds that are free of federal income tax and free of state taxes to residents. Some funds specialize in bonds from high tax states which are free of federal, state, and local taxes to residents. Bond issuers often reserve the option to recall the bonds—pay you off before the maturity date if interest rates drop. Non-recallable bonds are better but return is usually less. Cities can default and unless the bonds are insured, a bond fund is safer.

Annuities - Income is tax free until funds are withdrawn. Variable annuities allow *you* to select your own investments, usually among stock, bond and money market funds. Cautions: early withdrawal can be costly due to surrender charges and penalties. Even large insurance companies have failed, so be sure the company you're considering is rated financially strong by *all* prominent rating services.

Custodian Accounts - Open accounts for minor children at any bank or brokerage. Cash or securities can be transferred to such accounts without gift tax if less than $10,000 per child per year ($20,000 if spouse also contributes). Income from the account is taxable at the child's rate so long as it is not used to pay for the child's support. Income in excess of $1,100 is taxable at the parent's rate if child is under 14 years old (kiddie tax). Consider funding the accounts so that young children will earn $1,100 per year, adding more after children reach 14 years of age.

Helpful Hints on Buying Insurance

Protection from major misfortune is what insurance is all about. Considering the average worker earns over a million dollars before retiring, earning power is the greatest asset most persons have. The questions that should come to mind are: What will my family live on if I die or become disabled? If I'm found liable for someone's loss of life or earning power? Lose our house and all our possessions? But just as it is foolish to ignore such common perils, it's possible to be over-protected from them. The following are suggested income protection priorities and guidelines.

Medical

Coverage is often provided by the employer with the employer contributing part of cost. If not covered through work, purchase a plan through any group in which you have or can obtain membership. Health Maintenance Organizations (HMO) emphasize preventive care and provide the most comprehensive coverage at the lowest rates; the downside is that your choices of doctors, treatment and appointments are more limited. If an HMO or other group coverage is not available, purchase an individual policy through a large and reputable company. Keep premiums down by taking the highest deductible offered. Avoid one-illness policies like cancer insurance, or policies priced far below the competition. You can get by without dental coverage. If you cannot afford a comprehensive coverage, purchase a major medical policy where you pay all medical bills under say, $2000. The premium will be more affordable and you'll be protected from losing your life savings. Make sure any medical policy you buy is guaranteed renewable and is incontestable after a stated period (like two years).

Life

How much life insurance should you carry? None if no one is dependent on you. But if your family depends on your wages, you need some. A very rough rule of thumb is 5 - 7 times your annual take home pay, based on the assumption the surviving spouse can acquire the

137

Life . . .

necessary training and skills to support the family within that time. A better estimate can be calculated as follows:

1. Multiply current annual expenses by 50% to 75% (spouse only = 50%; spouse and child = 65%; spouse and 2 or more children 75%).

2. Get estimate of your annual survivor insurance benefits from Social Security Administration (current maximum for spouse and 2 children under 16 years is about $16,000; spouse and 1 child about $13,000, and about $7,000 for spouse over 62 years of age).

3. Estimate income or assistance your family can expect from other sources (spouse's earnings, financial help or housing from relatives and friends).

4. Estimate annual income from any savings or income producing assets you may have—or will soon inherit (use 8% of asset's value to estimate income).

5. Find the total amount the family can expect to receive (2 + 3 + 4 above).

6. Additional income required (1 - 5 above).

7. Amount of life insurance required (6 above ÷ .08).

The most life insurance coverage for the least cost is *term* insurance, purchased through a membership group or directly from reputable national companies. Term insurance rates increase with age. As your savings and assets increase, you should be able to cut back on the amount of term insurance needed, thereby keeping premiums near constant. Insurance companies usually offer the first five or ten years at attractive rates as an incentive to buy, so you may be able to lower your premium by shopping around and changing companies after the initial period. Term insurance does not have any cash value. Insurance policies which combine life insurance and cash value such as *universal, whole life,* and *single premium* policies are compromises that provide less life insurance per dollar than term policies and less return on the dollar than other savings options.

Disability

Even though the chances of becoming disabled are six times greater than those of dying, many persons do not have this important protection. While it's true that most workers are covered for job-related disabilities through *workers' compensation* and *social security,* these benefits are minimal, very restrictive and taxable. For example, social security benefits are not payable unless your disability is total and expected to last a year or result in death; worker's compensation is restricted to disabilities that are work-related and payments are modest.

If you are not covered by a disability policy through your employer, consider purchasing your own. Disability policies are more expensive than life insurance because of the higher probability of use. You can save on premiums by getting a group rate, and by extending the waiting period to six months. Policies that pay if you can't work in your usual occupation cost about 30% more than those which pay if you can't work in *any* job. Some disability policies cover your "own" occupation for several years and "any" occupation thereafter. Disability policies are sold on the basis of the amount of monthly benefit provided. Determine the amount needed by the same process used to determine life insurance needed, but use monthly instead of annual figures. Disability income you receive from personal policies for which you paid the premium is tax free.

Homeowner

There are three major types of homeowners insurance: basic, broad form, and all risk. The best value is usually the broad form which covers all the common perils at an affordable price. If you live in a flood or earthquake area, special insurance is recommended if you are in a government designated flood plain or earthquake zone; otherwise it's likely to be too expensive to be practical.

Homeowner . . .

Mortgage lenders require that you carry property insurance, but can't make you purchase such insurance from them. You'll probably do better with major companies that specialize in such insurance. Homeowners policies also provide coverage of furnishings, personal property, reimbursement for living costs while home is being repaired, and liability protection in the event someone gets hurt on your property.

It's important that the house itself be insured for at least 80% of its current replacement cost, otherwise the settlement will be based on the depreciated value of the loss rather than its replacement value—a BIG difference and not in your favor. Your insurance agent can supply the important current replacement cost figure, but it's simply the total square footage multiplied by the current cost per square foot of building a comparable home in your area.

The standard policy provides replacement of the *contents* of the home on the basis of the depreciated value of each item. For a 10-15% increase in premium you can get replacement on the basis of full purchase price. By increasing the standard $250 deductible to $500 or $1,000 you could get the full replacement cost feature and lower the total cost of the policy. Most policies limit the coverage of valuables such as jewelry, collectibles, cameras, and office equipment. Purchase a "personal articles" rider if policy limits are too low for your possessions.

Auto

Like home insurance, car insurance is required by lenders. The high rates reflect the grim truth that our roads and highways are the most lethal part of our environment. That's also why most experts advise carrying no less than $1,000,000 liability and $50,000 property damage. To keep premium costs down, consider the following:

Auto . . .

Compare rates from several of the largest national auto insurance companies and membership groups. Avoid high risk cars. Rates are lower for cars that are less likely to get stolen, suffer less damage and are less expensive to fix. Check the model's record with your insurance agent before you buy. Drop any duplicate coverage like medical payments. Drop collision and comprehensive coverage on cars valued at less than $3,000; raise collision and comprehensive deductibles to $500 or $1,000 on expensive cars. *Caution*: when renting cars, you normally are responsible for damages up to the deductible amount on your own car policy, providing your policy doesn't exclude rental cars altogether. But, if you're carrying high deductibles, a small dent or windshield nick could cost you plenty. Buying the extra insurance from the rental company is expensive, $10 per day and more in some locations. A good solution is a premium credit card, such as a gold card, which covers collision and comprehensive damage to cars that are rented using the card. Don't file small claims (less than $500 or $1000). The insurance company will raise your premiums by as much as 25% or may even cancel your policy.

Liability

It's sad but true: as your wealth increases, so do your chances of being sued. All it may take for a big judgement against you is a careless act by you, a member of your family, or one of your employees. Even if you win in court, it can still cost you thousands in legal defense. Given that six-figure damage awards are commonplace, experts advise that the minimum amount of liability insurance coverage for an average homeowner and driver is a million dollars. The good news is that such coverage is surprisingly inexpensive. A typical million dollar "umbrella" policy costs under $200 a year. It may even be possible to offset this premium cost by increasing the deductibles on home and auto polices. Standard Business Owners Policies already provide $1,000,000 of liability protection. Owners of high risk property such as rental units or aircraft, often place such property in a corporation to further limit their personal liability.

Helpful Hints on Investing

Your Portfolio

Surprisingly, studies show that amateur investors do about as well as the professionals. That means that your guess is probably as good as anyone's, and maybe better. The important thing is to get started so the power of compounding is working for you. Time is a perishable asset you either use or lose. The following guidelines will help you start your investment portfolio.

Return On Investment: Regardless of the 10 year period selected, the ranking of return on investment, from best to worst, would be as follows:

- small company stocks (smallest 20% on NY stock exchange)
- large company stocks (S&P 500)
- long term corporate bonds (20-30 year)
- long term government bonds (20-30 year)
- cash equivalents (treasury bills, CD, bank notes)

That returns are directly related to risks involved is not surprising. The eye opener is that money invested in cash and bonds over the past forty years has barely kept ahead of inflation! Many investment managers are satisfied with returns averaging 2% above long term inflation. For instance, the average annual inflation rate over the past 40 years was a little over 4%, suggesting a reasonable return to expect during that period would have been least 6% per year. A portfolio composed of equal parts cash, bonds, and stocks of large companies would have yielded 7% and met the goal. Portfolios composed of fixed return investments (cash and bonds) would have yielded less than 5% and would have fallen short. *Caution*: Inflation figures are based on the consumer price index and are not immune to manipulation. For example housing and automobile purchases were dropped from the Index in recent years because they were not ordinary recurrent expenses. A cynic might observe that it also made the inflation rate appear lower compared to past rates. An independent study of the cost of food, medications, transportation and other necessities for persons on fixed incomes indicated the inflation rate for them was twice the official national rate.

Portfolio . . .

Allocation: To ensure a good return and prevent large losses in market swings, the portfolio should include stock, bond and cash investments. The recommended allocation among these investments depends on a person's stage in life, the amount and predictability of income and how comfortable the person is with risk. These factors are incorporated in the table shown in Figure 42, which can be used as a guide. Whatever the specific allocation, the lesson from the past is clear: to keep ahead of inflation, you must own something (stock in a company); if all you do is *loan* money to others to invest (cash and bonds), your savings aren't likely to reach the levels needed.

Diversification: Once the allocation of the portfolio is decided, the next step is to spread the investment over a number of companies so that failure of one doesn't endanger the entire investment. For the beginning investor, the best way to do this is to buy shares in mutual funds which are composed of scores of companies selected and monitored by experienced managers.

Mutual funds are usually offered as part of a family of stock, bond, and cash funds. Shifting money from one fund to another within the fund family can usually be done with a phone call. Many investors use two or more fund families for added choice and diversification. The major types of mutual funds, listed from highest to lowest risk and return, is shown in Figure 43. Notice that both allocation and diversification are achieved by investing in a mix of stock, bond and cash funds.

The track record of mutual funds is updated monthly in popular financial magazines. Look for no-load funds with good records over a 5 to 10 year period. The record shows that no-load (no sales charge) mutual funds have done about as well as mutual funds that have sales charges (commonly 2%-8%). Most funds charge a management fee that averages close to 1% per year.

Investor Characteristics	✔ BLOCK	Small Company Stocks	Large Company Stocks	Corp & Govt. Bonds	Cash Equiva- lents
Young to Mid Career Above Average Income Assured Income Comfortable With Risk	(I)	30%	45%	20%	5%
Mid to Late Career Average Income Stable Income Accepts Some Risk	(II)	15%	30%	45%	10%
Near or at Retirement Below Average Income Unstable Income Uncomfortable With Risk	(III)	5%	25%	65%	5%

Directions

Place a check mark next to the characteristics that apply to you. If three (3) checked characteristics are:

Located in any one block, use the allocation for that block. For example, 3 checks in block (I) the allocation would be: small stocks 30%; large stocks 45%; bonds 20% and cash 5%.

Divided between the blocks (I) and (II), the allocation would be: small stocks 20%; large stocks 40%; bonds 30%; cash 10%.

Divided between blocks (II) and (III), the allocation would be: small stocks 10%; large stocks 25%; bonds 55%; cash 10%.

Divided between blocks (I) and III), the allocation would be the same as block (II).

FIGURE 42 Guide For Portfolio Allocation

Portfolio . . .

Market Timing vs Buy and Hold: The economy tends to follow a broad cyclical pattern with some periods favoring stocks while others favor fixed return investments like cash and bonds. A system for predicting exactly when changes will occur has yet to be devised, but knowing what part of the cycle the economy is in can give investors an idea of what the next move should be (Figure 44).

Some feel that interest rates or computer tracking of hundreds of market indicators enable them to detect major market moves in time to re-allocate portfolio investments and capture additional profits. Thus far, however, the only proven long term strategy is the buy and hold approach, using a 10 year minimum for stock investments. Beginning investors are advised to trust in and stick with their basic allocation to provide a good return with minimum risk. Going after higher returns by radically changing allocation on the basis of market projections is best left to the more experienced and adventurous.

KIND *	COMPOSITION
Growth	Common stocks of small companies
Growth and Income	Common stocks of large and small companies
Income	Common stocks of large companies
Balanced	Mixture of common stocks and bonds
Corporate Bond	Bonds of domestic and foreign companies
Government Bond	Bonds and notes of national governments
Money Market	Cash equivalents: bank, corporate, and government notes

* *Listed from highest to lowest risk and return*

FIGURE 43 Major Kinds And Composition Of Mutual Funds

Dollar Cost Averaging: A strategy that reduces the risk of buying during a temporary high is called dollar cost averaging. By buying an equal dollar amount each week or month, you'll buy more shares when the price is low and less when the price is high, assuring that your shares are bought at the average price during the period. Many mutual funds offer convenient ways of buying a fixed dollar amount of shares each month.

Real Estate

Real Estate, in the form of a residence, normally represents a large part of a person's net worth. In the past, real estate has accounted for the accumulation of more wealth than any other single investment. The future outlook for profits, however, does not look as promising as the past. Aside from the current flat market, the downside is a long term investment with poor liquidity and high transaction costs. On the plus side is that home ownership still offers considerable tax advantages including deductible mortgage and equity loan interest, deferred gains and the exclusion of $125,000 gain from sale of residence by owners over 55 years of age. You can expect that in addition to providing shelter, your home will likely retain its value.

If you want additional real estate investments consider a second home or rental (preferably to a family member). Losses from rentals you manage are deductible from taxable income (up to $25,000 if adjusted gross income is under $100,000 and phased out between $100,000 and $150,000). More adventurous investors might look for deeply discounted second mortgages or properties offered at federal, state and county tax auctions.

If you want hands off and liquidity, consider Real Estate Investment Trusts (REIT) which are like mutual funds composed of real estate estate properties.

147

STAGE OF CYCLE	INDICATORS OF STAGE *	BEST INVESTMENTS TO		
		BE IN	BUY	SELL
RECESSION	Demand Slows Production Decreases Unemployment Rises Interest Rates Fall	Bonds	Stocks	Cash
RECOVERY	Demand Begins to Rise Production Increases Unemployment Falls Interest Rates Rise	Stocks	Cash	Bonds
EXPANSION	Demand Increases Product Increases Unemployment Decreases Interest Rates Climb	Stocks	Stocks	Cash
PEAK	Peak Demand Full Production Full Employment Interest Rates Peak	Cash	Bonds	Stocks

* *Best single indicator of stage change is the level and direction of interest rates. Historic peak highs were 12%-15%, lows were 5%-8%.*

FIGURE 44 Optimum Investments During Business Cycle

Fixed And Variable Annuities

The income earned in annuity investments is tax deferred until withdrawn so account balances build up fast. Sales costs can be eliminated by keeping annuity in force through the penalty period (usually 6 or 7 years). In fixed annuities the return is fixed at a rate guaranteed by the insurance company. These policies make sense for the fixed return asset of your portfolio so long as you won't need the money for several years. The "variable" annuities allow you to allocate and switch investments among a group of mutual funds. Either investment may be a good option when you've maximized contributions to other tax deferred accounts such as IRA and 401(k) plans. The downside is surrender charges, income taxes and penalties if you decide to liquidate early. At least one major investment company offers a variable annuity contract with no surrender charges (income tax and federal penalty still apply). Caution: Several major insurance companies have gone into receivership recently and more are on the edge. Stick to large companies that have been awarded the highest rating by *all* rating services.

Precious Metals

A traditional inflation hedge has been gold and silver in the form of coins, bullion, and collectibles. These are considered high risk investments which don't provide current income and have high sales and maintenance costs. Some suggest that up to 5% of net worth can be kept as a kind of insurance against calamities such as war or runaway inflation.

Limited Partnerships

Limited partnerships sell shares in a group of diversified assets such as rental property and equipment, oil and gas wells, and other assets which combine current returns with tax benefits. Although the investor's liability is limited to the money invested, these are long term, high risk investments with high sales costs that are difficult, if not impossible to liquidate.

Helpful Hints on Estate Planning

The purpose of estate planning is to maximize the amount that will be transferred to your heirs or persons and organizations of your choosing.

Wills and
Letters
of Instruction

A *will* ensures that your assets will be distributed according to your wishes rather than by a state formula. Professionally prepared wills are not expensive, under $100 for simple wills. Do-it-yourself wills are better than nothing, but don't save you much if all you need is a simple will and not recommended if you need a more complicated one. It's not worth the risk of having your will nullified due to a small technicality you overlooked. If you have a blended family, with children from previous marriages, a professionally prepared will is recommended.

A *letter of instruction* should be prepared stating the location of the will, insurance policies, financial papers and net worth statement, funeral arrangements, disposition of personal items, and what you wish done with your body and useable organs. The letter should also include the names and addresses of the executor, attorney, accountant, insurance agent, broker and other advisors, as well as persons responsible for carrying out your specific instructions.

A *"durable power of attorney"* for healthcare should be signed at the time your will is prepared. This power allows your spouse or close relative or friend to act on your behalf should you become incapacitated by illness or accident. Many persons also sign a "desire for a natural death," popularly known as a "living will." This order prevents medical authorities from resuscitating and connecting you to machinery to prolong your life. Families have learned that, once connected, such machinery can siphon away life savings while authorities squabble over the legality of pulling the plug on your life support equipment.

Estate Taxes

Currently, if your estate after debts, funeral, legal and administrative expenses, and bequests you plan to make, is less than $600,000, you will escape federal estate taxes. If your entire estate will be going to your spouse with no strings attached, it can be *any amount* and still avoid federal estate taxes. However, when your spouse dies, only $600,000 of his or her estate will escape tax. The tax on amounts over $600,000 are high, beginning at 37% and increasing with the size of the estate to 50%.

Many persons don't realize how close their estate may be to the federal tax-free limit. The reason is that estates are based on the *appreciated* value of their residence, and other property they may own or likely to inherit before their death. Estates also include proceeds from all *life insurance* policies owned by the deceased—*even though the beneficiary is someone else*. This includes policies provided by employers and membership groups some of which may pay double for accidental death. Many persons also overlook how fast inflation increases the dollar value of their holdings.

Estate taxes should not be confused with state inheritance taxes which, if they apply, are paid by the heirs not the estate. Check the inheritance laws in your state.

Here are some options for eliminating or reducing taxes when the estate exceeds $600,000:

Transfer Ownership of Assets: If one spouse owns most of the assets, some can be transferred to the other spouse so that the estate of each will be more balanced.

Create a Bypass Trust: A trust can be used to divide a couple's assets without having to transfer ownership of the assets. Called bypass or credit shelter trusts, they can be used as follows: each person's will provides that a trust be created upon their death and funded with up to $600,000 of their assets. Children, or other heirs, are named as the beneficiaries, but all the income from the

Estate taxes . . .

trust is paid to the spouse during the spouse's lifetime and the spouse may also use the principal if needed to meet living or medical expenses. The remainder of the estate, everything over $600,000, goes outright to the spouse and will be not taxable. The trust can also be made optional taking effect only if the surviving spouse thinks it necessary. In blended families, each parent can ensure that their natural children inherit their wealth after their spouse dies—by creating a Q-TIP (Qualified Terminal Interest Property) trust in their wills. The Q-TIP works much the same way as the bypass trust, but it is usually made irrevocable so it cannot be changed after the natural parent dies. By using trusts in this way a total of $1.2 million (2 X $600,000) can be sheltered from estate taxes.

Give Gifts: Each individual is permitted to give away $10,000 per year to as many individuals as he or she wishes. By each giving $10,000 in late December and $10,000 in early January, to 5 family members, it's possible for a married couple to reduce their estate by $200,000 in a week's time! What's more, paying for someone's tuition or medical expenses doesn't count against a couple's $20,000 per recipient limit. When one spouse dies, the survivor is restricted to $10,000 tax free gift per person per year, but the number of recipients remains unlimited. From a tax standpoint, if an asset has appreciated it would be better to transfer it as a bequest in your will rather than as a gift while you're alive. The reason is when the heir sells the property, the tax will be lower because the gain is based on the *appreciated* value of the bequest; whereas, when the recipient of a gift from a living donor sells the property, the gain is based on the donor's original cost which would result in a greater gain and higher taxes.

Charitable Donations: By making donations to charities, the estate reduced and the tax deduction can be used to reduce current taxable income. You can also create a charitable trust in which you continue to receive the income during your lifetime, and also be entitled to an immediate, although discounted, tax deduction.

Estate taxes . . .

Set up Insurance Trust: Proceeds from life insurance are not subject to income taxes, but are subject to estate taxes. You can eliminate insurance proceeds from your estate by creating an "Insurance Trust", provided you do so at least 3 years before your death (otherwise the IRS will nullify it). To create the trust you simply transfer policy ownership to the Trust. Your spouse can be named to receive income from the trust for life and when your spouse dies, the trust's funds could go to the children or other named beneficiaries. In this way, the trust shields life insurance proceeds from estate taxes on both your and your spouse's estates. The drawback is that you give up all rights to the policy (including borrowing its cash value or changing the beneficiaries) and the decision is irrevocable. Insurance trusts should be considered only when the estate value exceeds $1.2 million.

Set A Value of Family Business: The value of a family business may be set through an installment sale, or by a family partnership, whereby the parents' interest is fixed at the current income with any surplus going to children. Similarly, a family corporation can issue the owners a preferred stock having a fixed value and fixed return and issue the children non-voting common stock which increases in value with the growth of the business (up to $20,000 worth of common stock can be given to each child by the parent owners each year tax free). In this way the estate of the parents is kept relatively stable, growing assets are transferred to the children, and the parents retain control through their voting rights.

Probate

Probate (from the word probation) is a period for examining and proving a will. Depending on the state in which you live, and how efficient your executor and courts are, probate can mean a wait of six months to over a year before heirs get their inheritance. If the will is challenged, or involves property in more than one state, the process can take several years. Since probate records are public, anyone can find out how much you left and to whom. Lastly, your estate gets to pay for the cost of all this inconvenience, typically about 5% of the estate value.

Probate . . .

Now the good news. Any assets that are *jointly owned*, like residences and bank accounts, or *have named beneficiaries*, like insurance policies, pensions, profit share plans, IRAs, and Keoghs *escape probate* and are payable immediately. Realizing this, some seek to put <u>all</u> their property in joint names with rights of survivorship. However, this can extend liability exposure and increase estate taxes. A better solution is to create a "Revocable Living Trust" and put anything that would be subject to probate in that trust. Such trusts are very flexible. For example, you can keep all the income; you can change provisions or terminate the trust anytime, and you can be the trustee. However, because you have control over the property, the trust will be included in your estate for tax purposes. It's only the probate time, public exposure and cost that is avoided—but that's plenty. Check to see whether the probate laws in your state are particularly onerous. If so, and if a lot of your property will be affected, consider creating a Revocable Living Trust. Books are available for under $50 which provide all the necessary forms and instructions to establish such a trust.

blank forms

FINANCIAL SUMMARY

Category				QTR	YTD
Begin Balance					
INCOME					
EXPENSE					
GAIN (LOSS)					
End Balance					

BANK BALANCE						
MONTH						
STATEMENT BALANCE	DATE	AMOUNT	DATE	AMOUNT	DATE	AMOUNT
ADD DEPOSITS NOT SHOWN AND TOTAL 1. BELOW						
1.TOTAL DEPOSIT						
LIST ALL OUT-STANDING CHECKS AND TOTAL 2. BELOW						
2. OUTSTANDING						
END BALANCE (2 - 1)						

199_   ANNUAL SUMMARY

CATEGORY	YTD	ADJ	TAXABLE
Begin Balance			
INCOME			
EXPENSE			
GAIN (LOSS)			
End Balance			

199_ ANNUAL SUMMARY (Cont.)

ASSET	COST	PAID	CREDIT
TOTAL ASSETS			

CREDITOR	LOAN AMOUNT	REPAID PRINCIPAL	BALANCE
TOTAL LIABILITY			

OWNER	Contributions	Withdrawals	Balance

INVENTORY VALUE	Beginning	Purchased	Ending

INVOICE No. ____

DATE	OUR ORDER No.	YOUR ORDER No.

SOLD TO _____

SHIPPED TO (if other than SOLD TO) ____

SALESMAN	DATE SHIPPED	TERMS	SHIPPED VIA	PPD.	COLL.	F.O.B.

QUANTITY	DESCRIPTION	PRICE	AMOUNT

Thank You

⇦ PAY LAST AMOUNT IN THIS COLUMN

FILE

INVOICE No. _____

DATE	OUR ORDER No.	YOUR ORDER No.

SOLD TO _____

SHIPPED TO (if other than SOLD TO) _____

SALESMAN	DATE SHIPPED	TERMS	SHIPPED VIA	PPD	COLL.	F.O.B.

QUANTITY	DESCRIPTION	PRICE	AMOUNT

Thank You

PAY LAST AMOUNT
IN THIS COLUMN ⇨

PURCHASE ORDER

No. _____

DATE _____

TO _____

SHIP TO _____

REQUISITION No.	TERMS	SHIP VIA	DELIVERY DATE	F.O.B.

QUANTITY	DESCRIPTION	PRICE	AMOUNT

CHARGE TAX

TAX EXEMPT

Thank You

AUTHORIZED BY

PURCHASE ORDER

FILE

No. _____

DATE _____

TO _____

SHIP TO _____

REQUISITION No.	TERMS		SHIP VIA	DELIVERY DATE	F.O.B.

QUANTITY	DESCRIPTION			PRICE	AMOUNT

CHARGE TAX			
TAX EXEMPT		AUTHORIZED BY	

Thank You

PROFIT & LOSS STATEMENT
(From _____ To _____)

GROSS SALES $ _____

LESS RETURNS   (_____)

NET SALES   _____

LESS COST OF GOODS SOLD   (_____)

GROSS PROFIT FROM SALES   _____

OTHER BUSINESS INCOME   _____

INTEREST INCOME   _____

TOTAL INCOME   _____

LESS OPERATING COSTS   (_____)

NET PROFIT (BEFORE TAX)   _____

PERCENT OF TOTAL INCOME   _____ %

BALANCE SHEET
( )

ASSETS	LIABILITIES

ASSETS   LIABILITIES

CASH   **ACCOUNTS PAYABLE**

On Hand _____   _____
In Banks _____   _____   _____   _____

ACCOUNTS RECEIVABLE   **SHORT TERM NOTES**

_____   _____
_____   _____   _____   _____

INVENTORY   **TAXES**

Finished _____   _____
Partial _____   _____   _____   _____

PRE-PAID INSURANCE   **SALARIES & OTHER**

_____   _____
_____   _____   _____   _____

SUBTOTAL CURRENT   _____   **SUBTOTAL CURRENT** _____

FIXED ASSETS   **LONG-TERM DEBT**

Land   _____   Mortgages _____
Building _____   Notes   _____
Furnish _____   _____
Equip.   _____   _____
Less
Deprec. (_____)   _____   **OWNER EQUITY**   _____

TOTAL ASSETS   _____   **TOTAL LIABILITIES** _____

BUSINESS VALUATION
( )

1 INCOME

A. Total Income (less returns) _____

B. Total Expense (cost of _____
   goods sold plus operating
   less interest & depreciation)

C. Owner Salary (for a Sole _____
   Proprietorship, what a
   manager would be paid)

D. Income (A - B + C) _____

2 ASSETS & CAPITAL

A. Building & Land _____

B. Furnishings _____

C. Equipment _____

D. Inventory (raw & finished) _____

E. Other _____

F. Total Assets _____

G. Working Capital (current _____
   assets less current liabilities)

H. Assets & Capital (F + G) _____

3 EARNINGS

A. Income (1D) _____

B. Alternate Return (2H X _____
   current interest: inflation
   plus 4%)

C. Earnings (A - B) _____

4 MULTIPLE

A. Income (0 = unsure _____
   5 = assured)

B. Competition (0 = high _____
   5 = none)

C. Company (0 = start-up _____
   5 = known)

D. Industry (0 = decline _____
   5 = growth)

E. Multiple (A + B + C + D/4) _____

5 VALUE

A. Assets (2F) _____

B. Earnings Multiple (3C X 4E) _____

C. Market Value (A + B) _____

PERSONAL NET WORTH
(   )

ASSETS		LIABILITIES	
CASH		**CURRENT PAYABLES**	
On Hand	_____	On Hand	_____
Checking	_____	Credit	
Savings	_____	Cards	_____
CV Insurance	_____	_____	Other	_____	_____
SECURITIES		**SHORT-TERM LOANS**	
CD	_____	Bank	_____
Stocks	_____	Broker	_____
Bonds	_____	Credit	
Other	_____	Cards	_____
Bus. Equity	_____	_____	Other	_____	_____
PERSONAL PROPERTY		**LONG TERM LOANS**	
Auto(s)	_____	Auto(s)	_____
Furnish	_____	Home	
Jewelry	_____	Improve	_____
Other	_____	_____	Education	_____	
		Other	_____	_____
REAL ESTATE			
Home	_____	**MORTGAGES**	
Vacation	_____		
Rental	_____	Home	_____
Land	_____	_____	Vacation	_____
		Rental	_____
		Land	_____
RETIREMENT FUNDS			
		OTHER	_____
IRA	_____		_____	_____
SEP/Keogh	_____		
401 (k)	_____		
Annuities	_____		
Profit			
Share or			
Pension	_____	_____		
TOTAL ASSETS	_____	**TOTAL LIABILITIES**	_____	_____

NET WORTH (TOTAL ASSETS - TOTAL LIABILITIES)   _____

thanks

I am indebted to the authors of the numerous explanatory articles and books that have contributed to my understanding of the subject and whose ideas are reflected in the guidelines and suggestions offered here. The book would also not have been possible without the assistance and encouragement of associates and friends such as Tom Williams, CPA, for his guidance on accounting and tax matters; Dixon Brady for his whimsical illustrations; Diane Alexander, my wife, for her patience and editorial comments; Brenda Benfield and Suzanne Bucciarelli for typing and camera ready copy. I would be remiss if I didn't also mention Dolci and Bugs, our cats, who trekked across the ~~~***iiiiiii keyboard to posts atop monitor and printer in a daily demonstration of their support. And lastly, I must thank you, reader, for investing in this book. The ball is back in your court now; I hope you hit it big and *Account for Your Own Success!*

index

index

—— Updates ——

A update, including changes in tax law, is available each January by sending $1.00 together with self-addressed, stamped envelope to:

MCS, INC. • P.O. Box 4884 • Alexandria, VA 22303